"Our world glimmers with false hopes, offering financial gains, political power, and earthly efforts as conduits of blessing that promise much but fail to provide the peace and unity we desire. We need a better hope if we want to persevere. Thankfully, Irwyn Ince's new book *Hope Ain't a Hustle* wisely guides us through the book of Hebrews, reminding us that the object of our hope—Jesus himself—is the power of our endurance."

Melissa Kruger, author and vice president of discipleship programming at The Gospel Coalition

"This wonderful book is a pastoral, homiletical gift to those in need of encouragement. Diagnosing the problem of our era as a failure of hope, Irwyn Ince shares the fruit of his profound meditations, study, and preaching of the book of Hebrews. This is the kind of strong medicine needed to restore hope in a generation that has been disappointed by apathy, injustice, and scandal. He shows us that the hope of the gospel is the secret to joy and endurance. For those who are discouraged, sorrowful, and struggling, this wise book helps us to have eyes to see the beauty of Jesus anew."

Tish Harrison Warren, Anglican priest and author of *Prayer in the Night*

"In these difficult days, we all need more hope—not wishful thinking but solid confidence in the promises of God. In this richly biblical, deeply personal book, Irwyn Ince helps us persevere when times are tough. Ince's culturally relevant exposition of Hebrews—enlivened by stories from his own life and ministry—inspires more hope in the healing and reconciling power of the gospel."

Philip Ryken, president of Wheaton College

"For too long the American church has undermined the credibility of its witness by expressing good news for some but not all in and through local churches otherwise segregated by color, class, and culture. Indeed, it's long past time for Christ-followers to express a gospel of peace and hope for all people, not just some people, in more than words. In *Hope Ain't a Hustle*, my good friend Irwyn Ince provides both the biblical why and how for doing so as well as outcomes we can anticipate by taking intentional steps, as individuals and collectively, toward such ends."

Mark DeYmaz, founding pastor of Mosaic Church of Central Arkansas and author of *Building a Healthy Multi-ethnic Church*

"In a world where tactics of control, manipulation, and polarization appear to be the way to get ahead, Irwyn Ince posits the audacity of hope as an antidote to hustle culture. Grounded in the book of Hebrews and the life of Jesus, Ince reminds us Christian hope is secure, not just for individuals but also for a divided church and groaning world. Read this book for its clear-eyed hope amid our disenchanted world."

Ashley Hales, director of research at the Willowbrae Institute and author of *A Spacious Life*

HOPE
AIN'T A
HUSTLE

*Persevering by Faith
in a Wearying World*

IRWYN L. INCE JR.

FOREWORD BY CHRISTINA EDMONDSON

An imprint of InterVarsity Press
Downers Grove, Illinois

InterVarsity Press
P.O. Box 1400 | Downers Grove, IL 60515-1426
ivpress.com | email@ivpress.com

InterVarsity Press® is the publishing division of InterVarsity Christian Fellowship/USA®. For more information, visit www.intervarsity.org.

Scripture quotations, unless otherwise noted, are from The Holy Bible, English Standard Version, copyright © 2001 by Crossway Bibles, a division of Good News Publishers. Used by permission. All rights reserved.

While any stories in this book are true, some names and identifying information may have been changed to protect the privacy of individuals.

Published in association with the literary agent Don Gates of The Gates Group, www.the-gates-group.com.

The publisher cannot verify the accuracy or functionality of website URLs used in this book beyond the date of publication.

Cover design: David Fassett
Interior design: Jeanna Wiggins
Cover images: Getty Images: © oxygen, © Liyao Xie

ISBN 978-1-5140-0574-3 (print) | ISBN 978-1-5140-0575-0 (digital)

Printed in the United States of America ♾

Library of Congress Cataloging-in-Publication Data
Names: Ince, Irwyn L., Jr., 1968- author.
Title: Hope ain't a hustle : persevering by faith in a wearying world /
 Irwyn Ince ; foreword by Christina Edmondson.
Description: Downers Grove, IL : IVP, [2024] | Includes bibliographical
 references.
Identifiers: LCCN 2023036346 (print) | LCCN 2023036347 (ebook) | ISBN
 9781514005743 (print) | ISBN 9781514005750 (digital)
Subjects: LCSH: Hope–Religious aspects–Christianity.
Classification: LCC BV4638 .I525 2024 (print) | LCC BV4638 (ebook) | DDC
 234/.25–dc23/eng/20230928
LC record available at https://lccn.loc.gov/2023036346
LC ebook record available at https://lccn.loc.gov/2023036347

30   29   28   27   26   25   24 | 12   11   10   9   8   7   6   5   4   3   2   1

FOR AIDA MARGARET AND INDHIRA JELANI EKUNDAYO

My beautiful granddaughters,

as you grow may you always know

the full assurance of hope in a wearying world.

CONTENTS

FOREWORD

Christina Edmondson

"Head in the clouds."

"Unrealistic."

"Naive."

"Bamboozled."

"Ignorant."

"Heavenly minded and no earthly good."

There are a lot of misconceptions and mislabeling of the truly hopeful among us. In a world that is marred by sin, shame, and cynicism, the hopeful person can almost be seen as useless, insincere, and insensitive at worse. As a pleasant realist, I have had these thoughts and judgmentally called or whispered those names myself. I imagine the root of the name-calling and frustration may be that on some level people believe hopefulness requires a detachment from the truth. The realist or pessimist may look at the one known for hopefulness as employing some type of selective dissociation from reality, especially tough realities, in order to be hopeful. Under this thinking, someone is hopeful because they are in denial of the fierce realities of pain, suffering, and oppression. However, after trials and reflection, I'd argue that it is the hopeful person who is most committed to truth: the truth of what is truly happening in the moment and the truth of the possibilities of what is to come.

My first counseling supervisor at the University of Rochester was the late Dr. Susan Horowitz. She would often tell me alongside my friend and fellow intern that at times we would need to "hold the hope" in the room for our clients. Too often people who had entered into counseling or family therapy were standing on their last legs holding on with shaky hands to a marital vow or vision for their family, past and present. As we attempted to apply the best of our clinical training to the very real and intense issues they presented, we were also charged with something that was beyond our studies. Susan, a woman who was quite familiar with the Old Testament prophets, pushed us within our secular program to be the holders of Hope.

This hope and the idea of holding it was never meant to be a substitute for or diminisher of wisdom, peer-reviewed research, and hard work. However, hope was the fuel that made all those other things receivable and attractive to our weary clients. Oftentimes clients have been told that if they work some relational formula, things would be okay, yet they found themselves on the verge of divorce. Clients who had shepherded children into the world only to be estranged from those children in the present moment felt the crushing pains of hopelessness. How in the world would they go on?

The same is true in the church, as I think about both congregants and pastors I have served through the years who are feeling the weight of deep depression and anxiety, unfulfilled dreams, spiritual abuse and invisibility, unrelenting criticism, and disappointments. How can they go on? It is not just the preached restating of a promise of a brighter tomorrow and future, but they also need endowed and contagious hope to go forward: a hope that would help them to live out this admonition from the old saints to run on a little while longer to see what the end is going to be. It takes hope to run even toward a known ending.

Nevertheless, undirected or blanketed hopefulness is risky business. Like in loving another human being, there are no guarantees of reciprocation, mutuality, or flourishing. However, the Christian's hope is, or ought to be, a directed or pointed one. It is a hope in a specific person: Jesus. As Dr. Ince will remind us in this book, hope is not a hustle. God is not interested in bamboozling us or toying with us as if God is some bored ancient Greek deity like Zeus orchestrating human suffering like a soap opera. God promises to bottle our tears, make right all injustice, and God will not mock us in our pain like some cruel bully or abusive parent. Jesus is Emmanuel, God with us, and never God mocking us. Our rightly directed hope does come with guarantees and better-stated promises that tend to our bubbling or raging anxieties in this life. We can trust Jesus and lean into hope in him.

The prophet Jeremiah offers words from the Lord that anchor him and the people of God then and now. He says in the often-quoted text found in Jeremiah 29:11 (NIV), "'For I know the plans I have for you,' declares the Lord, 'plans to prosper you and not to harm you, plans to give you hope and a future.'"

You would think that it would be enough just to have the plan to give us a redemptive future, a tangible outcome guaranteed and secured by the blood of the Lord Jesus Christ. But, in God's divine wisdom, he knows that his people not only need an outcome that we can touch and feel one day but that we need hope to remind us that we will get there. How can we embrace the Lord's invitation and command to rest if we do not have the beauty of hope anchoring our souls along the way to a secured future? Without hope, we live tossed by the winds and reaction to the wilds of this world, and journey through a restless path toward a promised future. Yet, in God's kindness and mercy, our Heavenly Father has given to us hope and a future. We desperately need both.

Irwyn Ince, a pastor's pastor, offers us in this book an opportunity to experience honest, kind, and directive shepherding toward the reasonable and secure hope we have in Christ. My prayer is that as we pray and discern through these passages we will all mature a bit more in our Jesus-directed hope and find ourselves better equipped to face uncertain tomorrows until the glorious tomorrow is revealed.

HUSTLING OR HOPING?

In 2003, my oldest son and I took the Amtrak from the Baltimore/Washington International Airport Station to New York City's Penn Station. He was almost eleven at the time, and he was used to going to NYC. Brooklyn is my hometown and the borough of his birth. We moved to Maryland when he was two, so he only knew the city as a visitor.

The purpose of this particular trip was to move a legacy piano from my parent's Brooklyn house to our home in Maryland. My cousin, who lived in Brooklyn, did a little moving as a side gig on weekends. He and I were going to move the piano while our sons, who were similar ages, would spend some time together.

When my son and I arrived at Penn Station, we made our way from the Amtrak exit to the Metropolitan Transit Authority (MTA) entrance. As we stood at the machine to purchase MetroCards, I heard a voice behind me, a short distance away. "Yo, big man! Yo, big man!"

I'm not the largest of human beings, but I'm not small either. I had ridden the train in NYC for over thirty years and developed the necessary skill of ignoring people I didn't want to be bothered by. My son had not developed that skill. He tapped me on the side and said, "Dad, I think that guy over there is trying to talk to you." Exhaling, I turned to see what this dude wanted.

"Yo, I got MetroCards man. Whatever amount you need! Look, you either gonna give the money to me or to Bloomberg! And I need it more!"

He didn't exactly open his coat to display all kinds of items for sale, but that was the vibe. And you have to respect his pitch. I laughed on the inside when he said I was either going to give my money to him or to Mayor Michael Bloomberg. He would charge me less for a MetroCard than if I went with the legal way of obtaining a card through the machine.

This, my friends, is called a hustle. He was trying to make some money outside of the system. I have no idea how he obtained those MetroCards of varying values nor did I have any way of validating whether they had any money on them before I paid him in exchange for two cards.

"Do you take debit cards?" I asked him. "'Cause that's all I've got." With that, he went on his way to the next potential customer (or victim).

Growing up in a city like New York, you get used to a hustle. You might even end up doing a little hustling yourself. The hustler offers someone something of value, or something another person may desire. If you were to obtain this item through the prescribed means, it would cost you much more than what the hustler is selling it for. You might not even be able to afford it.

Typically, the first question you ask yourself isn't about the morality of the transaction. *Should I buy this even though I don't know how it was obtained?* No. Our first concern is around the issue of trust. *Can I trust the hustler? Am I going to be the victim of a hustle?*

There was no way I was going to trust that gentleman with my money. I turned back to the machine and purchased cards for my son and me so we could make our way to Brooklyn. I was used to this kind of hustle and knew it wasn't worth the risk of hoping to get a better deal from the MetroCard hustler. It's one thing to deal with MetroCards. It's quite another matter to hold on to hope in the face of circumstances that communicate to us that this hope might be a hustle.

The particular hope I'm referring to is the Christian hope of experiencing an embodied life of being knit together in love across lines of deep division and difference. If you ask people what they hope for, you might hear answers like peace, justice, health, and happiness. But God makes a distinct promise in the Bible that seems out of reach in our current cultural moment. This promise is the reunion of humanity under the lordship of Jesus Christ. It is the promise of setting all things right. It is the promise that he will renew the whole world such that nothing and no one will ever be wrong again.

In his book *Love Your Enemies*, Arthur Brooks describes America's current age as a culture of contempt, one in which we are siloed into echo chambers that reinforce our positions and encourage us to hold in contempt those whose views differ from ours. And it is not simply that our contempt is directed toward views. Our contempt is aimed at those who hold them. Their views are not what is worthless—they are worthless. Brooks writes with respect to the broader political culture, but his assessment also applies in a narrower way to the church in America. Christians are also beset with this culture of contempt. All you have to do is spend a little bit of time on social media to experience this contempt at work.

In their 2016 article "Americans Struggle to Talk Across Divides," Barna Group research points out,

> The United States is in a cultural crisis. There are gaping fissures between the rich and poor, growing tensions between races, disunity among faith groups, increasing resentment between genders, and a vast and expanding gap between liberals and conservatives. Generation, gender, socioeconomics, ethnicity, faith, and politics massively divide the American population. . . . "This splintering and polarization of American culture has made it more difficult than ever to have a good conversation, especially about faith," says David Kinnaman, president of Barna Group and the lead designer and analysis on the study. "Even when two people agree, honest interaction can seem elusive. Try to talk about things like gay marriage—or anything remotely controversial—with someone you disagree with and the temperature rises a few degrees. But being friends across differences is hard, and cultivating good conversations is the rocky, up-hill climb that leads to peace in a conflict-ridden culture."[1]

It can be argued that from the time sin entered the human predicament in Genesis 3, humanity has lived in a conflict-ridden cultural context. It is true that there is nothing new under the sun (Ecclesiastes 1:9). Yet, in every age the conflicts in culture take a particular shape. Today's climate is a culture of contempt that can cause Christians to forsake their hope for the experience of shalom across dividing lines.

With its deep divides in the American church, our current culture of contempt makes it difficult to hold on to hope. What we are called to grasp is that hope is woven into the fabric of the Christian faith. Not hope as an idea or a wish but hope as a confident trust in God and his promises. This hope drives us to a disposition toward others that begins with respect.

In January 2020, our Institute for Cross-Cultural Mission held a Clergy Story Table event in Washington, DC. I facilitated our conversation on the issue of racial justice and the church. We brought together a diverse local group of ten pastors for this purpose. They were ethnically diverse (African American, Korean American, Venezuelan, and Anglo American), and they were theologically diverse (Baptist, Mennonite, Methodist, and Presbyterian).

Our conversation was honest and sometimes raw. One sentiment shared, particularly by two of the African American pastors, was that they believed the visions of Revelation 5:9-10 and 7:9-12 will come to pass one day, but they do not expect to experience the reality of it in their local churches today.

"I don't trust that white people are serious about reconciliation and justice issues. They're not willing to pursue it unless they are in control." The temptation in this current moment, particularly for ethnic minorities, is to stay in and focus on their ethnic ecclesial spaces. A pastor friend recently told me, "I just feel like going back into all-Black everything." I understand this frustration personally. The focus on race, justice, and even reconciliation in Christian circles brings with it accusations of bowing to Critical Race Theory, Marxist ideology, or "Wokeness." The polarization is deep.

So what does a robust embrace of Christian hope look like in practice? In her book *Unfettered Hope,* Marva Dawn writes,

> We use the English noun and verb *hope* in many ways—to signify what we anticipate or expect, what we would recommend if we could control things, what we most earnestly desire or wish for if we could have our own way, or what we truly believe in or in what or whom we have confidence.[2]

The pastors who told me they do not expect to experience the kind of reunion of humanity across these lines of deep difference are expressing a lack of hope. Holding on to this kind of aspiration can feel like an exercise in futility. It can feel like a hustle. And who wants to be on the wrong end of a hustle?

But God is not a hustler. And the hope he calls us to cannot be built on naive expectations that people will start seeing things the way we do. Our longing cannot be built on the arrogant assumption that we are completely right in the positions we take. It cannot even be built on an expectation of steady improvement. If the arc of the moral universe does indeed bend toward justice, that arc will never be smooth and straight from a human perspective. It will have twists and turns, ups and downs, starts and stops. Our hope, if it is to be enduring, must be rooted in the glory of Jesus Christ.

This kind of hope is enabling for how we live and is embodied in our daily decisions—and that is what this book is about. It's about an enduring hope that's able to carry us through the aspects of life that make it seem as though we are being hustled.

The New Testament book of Hebrews will be the primary biblical guide for our journey. The recipients of that extended pastoral exhortation were hoping for an end to their suffering for following Jesus Christ. They earnestly desired relief. In an attempt to take control and secure that relief, they were willing to compromise their faith.

Their pastor told them that they had need of endurance (Hebrews 10:36). He didn't just point them to some kind of wishful thinking. He pointed them toward the present reality of Jesus Christ, the great high priest, seated at the right hand of the Majesty on high. Because of this, they weren't waiting around for the "sweet by and by" to arrive. They were called to a life now that demonstrated the longing and ambition they had been brought into. It was a life of striving for peace with everyone and striving for holiness (Hebrews 12:14). It meant not allowing a "root of bitterness" to grow up among them in their relationships with others (Hebrews 12:15).

Are you experiencing hope fatigue? Are you wearied by our culture of contempt? Are you exhausted by being in a continual state of outrage? I invite you to walk with me in this exploration of Christian hope as the ultimate antidote for the fatigue, weariness, and exhaustion engendered by our current climate. This hope is not a hustle.

In the pages that follow, we will discover that living in a broken and imperfect world means that threats to our deepest longings for peace are the norm. Jesus tells his disciples in John 16:33 that in him they have peace, and in the world they have tribulation. What are they to do in the face of the norm of trouble? Take heart, he says, "because I have overcome the world." Taking heart is the language of hope. We will press forward from the norm of trouble to the paradox of hope.

It's not just that threats are normal, it's that hope seems unreasonable. In his exhortation to the Corinthians about the assurance of their resurrection in Christ's resurrection, the apostle Paul explains, "If in Christ we have hope in this life only, we are of all people most to be pitied" (1 Corinthians 15:19). Christian hope seems unreasonable because very often we will not experience victory in this life. Christian hope informs this life by being a forward-facing and upward-gazing perspective as our great high priest intercedes for us.

Last, we will tease out the implications of Christian hope for our individual lives and our lives together as God's people. Hear Paul again, this time as he introduces his letter to Titus. He is "an apostle of Jesus Christ, for the sake of the faith of God's elect and their knowledge of the truth, which accords with godliness, in hope of eternal life, which God, who never lies, promised before the ages began" (Titus 1:1-2). Those who have hope of eternal life strive for godliness in this life, individual and corporate, for the benefit and blessing of others. Hope is the necessary means of our endurance, bearing witness to Christ in a divisive world.

PART 1

THE STORM
BEFORE
THE CALM

1

LIVING IN THE DANGER ZONE

Before we determine how to live in a world where
our highest hopes are not satisfied, we must ask,
What does one do under such circumstances?

DR. MARTIN LUTHER KING JR.,
"SHATTERED DREAMS"

I was introduced to the CrossFit fitness training method in 2010. CrossFit is "constantly varied functional movement performed at high intensity."[1] There are several benchmark workouts known simply as "the girls." There's Annie, Barbara, Cindy, Diane, Elizabeth, Fran, Grace, Helen, Jackie, Kelly, Linda, Mary, and Nancy.

Why female names for these benchmark workouts? Well, it doesn't have much to do with gender. These workouts are named after hurricanes. CrossFit decided to follow the pattern of the National Weather Service, which started to assign female names to storms after 1953 because they believed "short, distinctive given names in written as well as spoken communications is quicker and less subject to error."[2] Greg Glassman, the founder of CrossFit, wrote, "This convenience and logic inspired our granting a special group of workouts women's names, but anything that leaves you flat on your back and incapacitated only to lure you back for more at a later date certainly deserves naming."[3]

These workouts are just like hurricanes. There's a calm before the storm. You're feeling fine, talking with your fellow gym members after the coach has taken you through a nice warm-up, getting you ready to work out. Then she starts the timer, counting down to the start of the workout. "Ten seconds!" she yells. "3-2-1, go!" are the next words out of her mouth and all hell breaks loose. At a certain point, you feel as though you might die. If you can think at all, you're asking yourself, *Why am I here, doing this voluntarily?* The workout ends and you wonder, *Am I dead?* The devastation in the gym is evident as people lay on the floor all over the place, making sweat angels.

This is just what happens in a hurricane. There's calm, and then there's the realization that the storm has hit and you are no longer in control. Once the storm passes, there's chaos. Devastation is all around.

What we discover in the opening chapter of the book of Hebrews is a reversal of that order. There is a storm taking place in the Pastor's congregation.[4] Persecution and suffering are a reality in their lives. Their world has turned upside down. Because of this they are losing hope, tempted to drift away from their faith in Jesus Christ. They want a release from the pressure. Following Jesus is more costly than they had anticipated. They're asking, "Is it worth it?" They're in the height of the workout, when the pressure is most intense, and they want to quit. But they need to endure. The Pastor will say to them in Hebrews 10:35-36, "Therefore do not throw away your confidence, which has a great reward. For you have need of endurance, so that when you have done the will of God you may receive what is promised."

What is interesting, though, is how he begins to address their concerns. He wants them to endure, not to give up. But he does not start out his letter, his sermon, by saying, "Hold on," "Don't be discouraged," or "Keep the faith." These are all statements he will make later in the letter. But his starting point is with the unrivaled glory, majesty, and authority of the Son of God. The supremacy of Jesus Christ is their source of eternal hope in a topsy-turvy, upside-down world.

Key to the concept of hope are our earnest expectations, desires, and wishes. Not only that, but it is commonly understood that what we desire is *good* hope. Indeed, in the New Testament the noun and verb for hope, as well as their derivatives, "never indicate a vague or a fearful anticipation, but always the expectation of something good."[5] In the book of Hebrews, hope is intimately connected to covenant. The Pastor refers to covenant more than all the other writers of the New Testament combined. The word is directly used or implied twenty-five times in Hebrews.[6]

You see, every one of us faces the dangerous reality of having to live in a world where our highest hopes are not satisfied and often dashed. As Dr. Martin Luther King Jr. asked, "What does one do under such circumstances?" How do we live with good hope in the danger zone of unfulfilled expectations? When the things that we earnestly desire or wish for if we could have our own way remain out of reach? When what we truly believe in seems to be a lie? When we realize that the world is full of chaos?

CHAOS

There is perhaps no other chapter in the Bible that displays the divinity of Jesus Christ more strongly than the first chapter of Hebrews. You cannot read it and conclude that the Bible declares Jesus to be a mere prophet. No. He's God. The message is that the only way you will be able to keep hope alive is if you are clear on who Jesus is.

You see, there's a question that I have not posed yet: how do we know that what we're hoping for is what we *ought* to be hoping for? No encouragement to keep the faith is going to have any teeth unless we are gripped by the incomparable glory of Jesus the Christ. Make no mistake about it—unless your heart is beating to the rhythm of the grandeur, the bigness, the glory of Jesus, you'll never think that being a Christian is worth it.

The letter begins almost like the opening words to Star Wars, "Long ago in a galaxy far far away . . ." But this is no sci-fi tale. The first thing the Pastor wants to remind us of is that God has spoken.

Long ago at many times and in many ways, God spoke to our fathers by the prophets.

At various times in history and in different ways, God raised up and anointed prophets to declare his word with authority: Abraham, Moses, Samuel, Elijah, Elisha, Isaiah, Jeremiah, Ezekiel, Daniel, Hosea, Joel, Amos, and on and on for centuries. God spoke to his people through the prophets to direct them to himself. It was always so that they would know what was necessary for them to honor and glorify him. When he spoke, he said all that he wanted to say. He didn't leave out anything that was necessary.

God has not been silent, but we are often deaf. He spoke so that we would know him and understand who he is. Still, as glorious as the word spoken through the prophets was, it was varied, diverse, and fragmented because the prophets were many in number. A change took place when Jesus came on the scene. In these last days, the Pastor says, God has spoken to us by his unique and only Son.

When God the Son took on human flesh and was born of woman, born under the law, to redeem those who are under the law (Galatians 4:4), Jesus' word became the final, complete, full Word of God. That's why he says in the first verse of Hebrews 2, "Therefore, we must pay much closer attention to what we have heard, lest we drift away from it." If the word of the various prophets was glorious and authoritative, how much more glorious and authoritative is the message given to us by Jesus? God's word to *us* in Christ has been spoken fully and finally. "These last days," then, are the days of fulfillment—despite what life around us looks like.

In other words, God has upped the ante. The Son is far superior to the prophets. This first verse sets the tone and theme of the whole letter. Jesus is supreme over everything that came before him—prophets, priests, and kings. It all pointed toward him. He is the full and final Word of God.

He is not just one of the prophets. He is the heir of all things. His inheritance is the whole world. He came to lay claim on the whole creation as his own possession because he is the one through whom the world was created. He is the glorious radiance and exact imprint of God's essence. He is God and he makes the glory of God visible to us. That's why Jesus could say to his disciples, "Whoever has seen me has seen the Father" (John 14:9).

Who else but God upholds the universe by his powerful word? What the Pastor is telling his people is their Savior is the one who carries the universe along to its stated goal. Can you see why, when encouraging Christians to endure, the Pastor begins with Jesus' glory? You almost have to ask how the description could possibly get any better. What more could you say to describe how glorious Jesus is? But then you read the second part of verse 3.

> After making purification for sins, he sat down at the right hand of
> the Majesty on high.

In these few words, he lets us know that Jesus is not only the glorious prophet, but also the glorious priest. Just like the comparison between God's word through the prophets and God's word through the Son, there is a comparison between the ongoing work of the Old Testament priests and the final work of the great high priest Jesus Christ.

In the Old Testament, God appointed Aaron as the first high priest. All the priests came from his lineage. Their basic job description was to offer sacrifices in the presence of God on behalf of the people to cover the sins of the nation. This was necessary because God in his mercy had chosen a people for himself. He promised them, "I will be your God, and you will be my people" (cf. Exodus 6:7; Leviticus 26:12; Jeremiah 24:7; 2 Corinthians 6:16; Hebrews 8:10). The problem is that all people are sinners and disobey God, and God will not dwell in the midst of sin. The reality of his holiness demands that sin be dealt with if anyone is going to be in his presence.

In the Old Testament, God provided a line of priests whose daily ministry was to atone for their own sins and the sins of the people by sacrificing lambs and bulls and goats.[7] It was a gory and gruesome scene. Blood flowed in the tabernacle every day. That is how seriously God takes sin. He reminds them in Hebrews 9:22, "Without the shedding of blood there is no forgiveness of sins."

Every day blood was shed so the people would not be consumed. God's punishment for sin fell on lambs and bulls and goats. But as the Pastor says in Hebrews 10:4, "It is impossible for the blood of bulls and goats to take away sins." The blood of bulls and goats could never finally, fully, and completely take care of the problem of sin. So, the same sacrifices had to continually be offered over and over again.

But when the one who is the radiance of the glory of God came, he came as the Lamb of God who takes away the sins of the world. Jesus came as the unblemished, spotless Lamb of God. He came both as the sacrificial offering and the offeror. He is the great high priest who offered himself as the only one who could crush sin. As he was beaten and whipped, as the blood flowed from his head, his hands, his feet, purification was made for the sins of everyone who puts their trust in him. It is as the hymn writer says,

> See from His head, His hands, His feet,
> Sorrow and love flow mingled down:
> Did e'er such love and sorrow meet,
> Or thorns compose so rich a crown?[8]

Jesus made final and complete purification for sins. How do we know that it's final and complete? What was missing in the tabernacle when the priests went in to offer the blood of atonement? The chair! They had to stand daily offering the sacrifices. There was no chair because there was no rest. But when Jesus made purification for sins, the Bible says that he took his seat. The work was finished. There no longer remains any need of further sacrifice for sin.

Often our struggle to endure with hope is connected to our inability to cleanse our communities by our own efforts. We don't have the ability to permanently cleanse anything, even our own bodies! And we're unable to make anything or anyone spotless enough to appear before God.

The Pastor is showing his readers that Jesus is the glorious priest because they're being tempted to take matters into their own hands. They're tempted to make up their own way of salvation, and his message is that Jesus is the only one who can make the impure pure. The best place to find ourselves is in Jesus, not only because Jesus is the glorious prophet and the merciful high priest, but he's also the great and glorious king. The fact that he sat down tells us that he has completed his work of purification for sins and that he is the supreme king and judge. He didn't sit down in any old place, but at the right hand of the Majesty on high.

Jesus prayed to the Father in John 17:4-5, "I glorified you on earth, having accomplished the work that you gave me to do. And now, Father, glorify me in your own presence with the glory that I had with you before the world existed." He completed his work and was restored to his rightful position in heaven as the King of kings and the Lord of lords. Because of where he sits, we can only know him today as the glorious king by faith. He reigns supreme over heaven and earth.

But as Hebrews 2:8 tells us, "At present, we do not yet see everything in subjection to him." Fear, doubt, pain, oppression, hardship, and unbelief cloud our ability to see everything in subjection to him. The declaration that the Son is heir of all things, the exact imprint of God's nature, and the sustainer of the world is sweeping. There is truly no area of existence, material or immaterial over which he does not have absolute authority. This is meant to be a comfort to those who believe and a warning to those who don't. The Pastor is writing to people who claim to know Jesus. He loves them and is pained that some are drifting away because things are getting rough.

What I love about the Pastor is that he's not setting forth the divine nature of Jesus as an idea that's disconnected from life. He's not just giving them head knowledge. None of this rich theology about Jesus Christ is given in a vacuum. It is the epitome of theology applied to life. Jesus's divinity is important precisely because the world is full of chaos.

In verses 10-12, he quotes from Psalm 102:25-27:

Of old you laid the foundation of the earth,
and the heavens are the work of your hands.
They will perish, but you will remain;
they will all wear out like a garment.
You will change them like a robe, and they will pass away,
but you are the same, and your years have no end.

This is what God the Father says to God the Son. But why is he quoting Psalm 102? The psalm's heading from the Hebrew text is, "A Prayer of one afflicted, when he is faint and pours out his complaint to the Lord."

The psalmist is in the middle of a storm. Jerusalem has been destroyed and the temple is in ruins. He's overwhelmed by the chaos of this world. His world had been rocked. The temple was supposed to be the place where God made his name dwell. It was the evidence that the Lord was with his people. Now, what the psalmist thought was most secure and stable is gone. The Babylonians have crushed them and swept them into exile.

When I was young, my father worked at the World Trade Center. He usually took the train home to Brooklyn from work, but there were a few occasions when we drove into Manhattan to pick him up. I remember being parked outside waiting for Dad to come out and looking up at the towers through the car window. No matter how hard I strained my neck, I couldn't see the top. Those buildings amazed me. In my mind, they were permanent fixtures in New York City, as the pictures of the city skyline always included the Twin Towers.

Obviously, I was wrong as the towers fell on 9/11 and the city was thrown into distress.

The chaos reflected in the faces of New Yorkers that day recalls that of the psalmist.

For my days pass away like smoke,
> and my bones burn like a furnace.

My heart is struck down like grass and has withered;
> I forget to eat my bread.

Because of my loud groaning
> my bones cling to my flesh. (Psalm 102:3-5)

Then there's a turning point in verse 12 when he says,

> But you, O LORD, are enthroned forever;
>> you are remembered throughout all generations.

Amid the chaos that's around him, the psalmist realizes that the only stable, unchanging reality is that Yahweh, the Lord, is enthroned forever.

That's the message of Hebrews 1. The distress you feel is real, but the one who walked the streets of Jerusalem and said "Come to me all you who labor and are heavy laden, and I will give you rest" (Matthew 11:28) is none other than Yahweh, the Lord your God. He's telling them that Jesus is the one who laid the earth's foundations in the beginning, the one who created the heavens. Those created things will wear out, be rolled up like an old garment, and be changed, but the Lord continues forever. He is the same and his years have no end.

CALM

The glory of Jesus Christ enables calm while chaos is raging. We live in a nation divided and polarized politically, socioeconomically, racially, and on and on the list goes. But the Son loves righteousness and hates wickedness. Therefore he is anointed by God with the oil of gladness (Psalm 45:6-7; Hebrews 1:8-9).

What's so beautiful about the Pastor applying Psalm 45 to Jesus is that it is a wedding psalm. It describes the royal bride as she prepares to marry the king. Her heart overflows because her husband is the most handsome of men. Grace is poured on his lips. Her husband is the mighty one in

splendor and majesty. He rides out victoriously for the cause of truth and
meekness and righteousness.

But then the psalmist seems to go too far and says of the king, "Your
throne, O God, is forever and ever" (v. 6). The Pastor is letting us know
there's no problem at all because this psalm is really about Jesus. It is an
Old Testament view into the reality of the Trinity, one God in three
persons, Father, Son, and Spirit. The one who is addressed as God is
anointed by his God with the oil of gladness. Because of the Son's just and
righteous rule, because he loves justice and hates lawlessness, the Father
has such unsurpassed joy that he anoints the Son with the oil of gladness.

Jesus is the king and husband, and the church is his bride. He is the one
who is the most handsome of men. He is the one with grace on his lips.
He is the one who in splendor and majesty rules with absolute justice and
righteousness for the cause of truth. And those who are under his rule and
authority are the companions of those God describes in verse 9. His joy
and righteousness are the blessings he gives his companions.

The recipients of the letter to the Hebrews needed to hear that because
life seemed to be unjust. They were suffering persecution for their faith.
They needed to know that the justice of the Son overrules the injustice of
Rome. The justice of our Savior overrules the injustice of this world. That
reality is what empowers the people of God to endure ugly injustice and
to see beauty rise from its ashes.

When will we see righteousness and justice rule the day? Where is the
world going? The optimist says, "Things are getting better. As technology
advances we're improving the lives of people." The pessimist says, "Everything's going to hell in a handbasket!"

But Hebrews reminds us of where the world is really going. It's going
to the place where every knee will bow to Jesus. Creation is not under the
authority of angels. It's not under the authority of presidents and kings.
It's under the Son's authority.

That's why what he says in the last verse of the chapter is so encouraging: "Aren't the angels all ministering spirits sent out to serve for the

sake of those who are to inherit salvation?" Don't focus on the angels! They serve the Son. He sends them out to minister to his people!

I'm convinced that he says this not just to correct their bad theology, but to encourage them with the truth. There's a calm that comes after the storm. There's a day coming when God "will wipe away every tear from [his people's] eyes, and death shall be no more, neither shall there be mourning, nor crying, nor pain anymore, for the former things have passed away" (Revelation 21:4).

There's not only a calm that comes after the storm, but there's a calm that comes in the storm for the people of God. This truth becomes our comfort in the danger zone when our highest hopes do not seem to be satisfied.

2

CONSIDERING JESUS
IN THE DANGER ZONE

I gave to Hope a watch of mine: but he
An anchor gave to me.
Then an old prayer-book I did present:
And he an optic sent.
With that I have a vial full of tears:
But he a few green ears.
Ah Loiterer! I'll no more, no more I'll bring:
I did expect a ring.

GEORGE HERBERT, "HOPE"

In his poem "Hope," seventeenth-century poet and clergyman George
Herbert succinctly describes the dismay we experience when our hopes
remain unsatisfied. The speaker gives Hope three things: his watch, his
prayer-book, and his tears. Hope gives the poet three things in return:
an anchor, an optic, (a telescope), and a few green ears (unripe ears
of grain).

The speaker's gift of a watch says to hope, "Time's up! I've been waiting
far too long!" But Hope gives him back an anchor, as if to say, "Be
steadfast! You've got to wait a while longer." To demonstrate how patient
he's been, the speaker declares, "Look at my prayer-book! See how

faithfully I've been praying as I've waited for you to come to my aid!" But Hope has further counsel. "It's wonderful that you've been praying. Please continue. You don't need to stop praying. You need a telescope to help you to keep the long view in mind." In a final effort to sway Hope, the speaker brings his tears. "Do you understand how much I've suffered, and for how long? Can you grasp the depth of my pain and sorrow?" But Hope's gift of unripe grain says, "The day of harvest will come, when everything is made right. But it's not time yet."

Utterly frustrated, the speaker has given up on Hope. Hope's new name is Loiterer. "My expectations are dashed! You take too long for my tastes! In fact, I think you are an impostor. I'm going to have to look elsewhere for relief. I thought we were bound together in an intimate relationship. I expected you to give me a ring, signifying your commitment to me! But I'm left alone at the altar." But as Bruce Bryant-Scott points out, the ring isn't Hope's to give. All Hope can offer is patience.[1]

In his message "Shattered Dreams," Dr. Martin Luther King Jr. describes three unhealthy ways we attempt to live in a world where our highest hopes are dashed. One is responding with bitterness and resentment toward God, others, and even ourselves. This person "loves no one and requires love from no one. He trusts no one and does not expect others to trust him. He finds fault in everything and everybody, and he continually complains." This reaction "poisons the soul and scars the personality, always harming the person who harbors this feeling more than anyone else."

A second reaction is to withdraw and detach, not permitting others to enter our lives and refusing to enter the lives of others. "Too unconcerned to love and too passionless to hate, too detached to be selfish and too lifeless to be unselfish, too indifferent to experience joy and too cold to experience sorrow, they are neither dead nor alive; they merely exist."

The third option is fatalism, where people "succumb to an absolute resignation to that which they consider to be their fate and think of themselves as being little more than helpless orphans cast into the terrifying immensities of space." The fatalist, says Dr. King, becomes a puppet, not a person.[2]

The alternative to these destructive responses is the paradoxical "acceptance of unwanted and unfortunate circumstances even as we still cling to a radiant hope, our acceptance of finite disappointment even as we adhere to infinite hope."[3] Acceptance of unwanted and unfortunate circumstances sounds like fatalism. Ongoing disappointment, even if it's finite, makes us wonder, *Hope, where's my ring?* Hope is not an impostor. It can rightly be described as radiant and infinite. But what hope gives us in return for our longings is the exhortation to wait a while longer. It's not an exhortation to wait a while longer in misery, but with Jesus at the front of our minds.

We saw in the last chapter that life in the danger zone has to be lived under the lordship of Jesus, the glorious prophet, priest, and king. But there's more to say! Not only do we fix our attention on Jesus in his resurrection, but we also consider him in his incarnation. Biblical hope is not a disembodied, non-material hope. It is rooted in his incarnation. This hope is "creational, this-worldly, visible, physical, bodily hope."[4] The Pastor makes this clear when he says, "Since therefore the children share in flesh and blood, he himself likewise partook of the same things" (Hebrews 2:14).

THE OPEN GENERATION

In 2022, Barna Group published the results of a global research project on the spirituality of teenagers. The study included almost 25,000 teens (ages 13–17) from twenty-six countries and with sixteen different language translations for the questionnaire. They titled the three-volume publication *The Open Generation*, concluding this generation of teens is "open to different perspectives, different faiths and cultures." They want to

- open doors that shed light on entrenched inequity and injustice,
- air our stale systems that exclude and ostracize others, and
- make change—not just micro-change, but macro-change—and, more significantly, they believe they can do it.[5]

In volume one, *How Teens Around the World Relate to Jesus*, the researchers wonder what might come of their hope, their desire to make a difference in the world. Will the milestones, influences, or experiences of this life dampen the enthusiasm of this generation's teens?[6] Note that even asking questions like that express an expectation that reality will set in as these young image bearers grow older and experience how impossible it is to change the world for good. "How many teens may go on to join the growing number of 'church dropouts' or disenfranchised? How many may carry their winsomeness into adulthood?"[7]

Maybe you can relate to the enthusiastic hopefulness for change that is resonant in today's youth. Maybe you shared a similar disposition when you were younger. Have you fallen into one of the unhealthy responses to dashed hopes described by Dr. King, bitterness, withdrawal, or fatalism? More specifically, how do you respond to Jesus during unwanted and unfortunate circumstances?

It is interesting that teens across the globe generally consider Jesus trustworthy, generous, wise, and peaceful. The characteristics that make the top of the list for them are his forgiving and compassionate nature and his reputation as a teacher and miracle worker.[8] Simultaneously, there's a gap between their idea of a gentle, merciful Jesus and their sense of his relevance for them today.

There's a lagging sense that Jesus is personally and actively engaged in lives today. Generation-wide, there is little grasp of or belief in teachings about Jesus' incarnation, resurrection, and present-day relevance, even as teens applaud principles of his life and character. This reflects not only on teenagers but also on those who have taught or led them, especially in Christian circles. Have adults shown this generation how the principles they celebrate in Jesus' character also matter in everyday life?[9]

Here is the point: biblical hope is rooted in Jesus' incarnation! There can be little expectation that any generation is able to hold fast to the hope set before us (Hebrews 6:8) without delighting in and understanding the significance of the incarnation for our lives.

MADE LIKE US

In 1991 Gatorade launched what arguably became Michael Jordan's most iconic commercial ad, "Be Like Mike." Jordan was a household name all over the world and Gatorade capitalized on the fact that everybody wanted to "be like Mike" in some way. His athletic ability, his charisma, his wealth, his stardom. There was something about him that everyone wanted to be true about them.

At certain times in our lives, every one of us wants to be like someone. There's somebody we want to emulate. It could be a child who wants to be like their parent, an athlete who wants to pattern their style of play after a professional they admire, or a businessperson who sees the success of an executive or business owner. Perhaps we simply admire the integrity we see in someone else. Whatever the reason, there are people we aspire to be like. This is not necessarily a bad thing. In most cases, we're setting our aim high. If we become like this person, we'll be better than we are now. I doubt anyone aims to become worse than they are now.

In Hebrews 1, we discovered that Jesus is God. For the Son, there was nothing higher to aspire to. If he was going to be made like something other than he was, it was going to be a step down—a big step down. Whether you are contemplating the claims of the Christian faith, have recently come to embrace Christianity, or can hardly remember a time when you were not a Christian, what we are told about Jesus' incarnation is intended to move us to awe and wonder. The Pastor says in Hebrews 2:14 that since the children God gave to Jesus have a common humanity (they "share in flesh and blood"), Jesus joined himself to that same humanity. And then he gives us four reasons why Jesus was made like us.

To destroy the devil. "That through death he might destroy the one who has the power of death, that is, the devil" (Hebrews 2:14). When Jesus came, he didn't come with a sword in his hand, but he did come as a destroyer. He was made like us so that he could destroy the devil. The devil is real. We may have difficulty believing there is a powerful, utterly evil spiritual being whose power of death needs to be nullified and rendered ineffective. But Jesus clearly understood who Satan was and he didn't dismiss the devil or try to rationalize him away.

When he confronted the Jewish leaders in John 8 for not believing in him, he says,

> If God were your Father, you would love me, for I came from God and I am here. I came not of my own accord, but he sent me. Why do you not understand what I say? It is because you cannot bear to hear my word. You are of your father the devil, and your will is to do your father's desires. He was a murderer from the beginning, and has nothing to do with the truth, because there is no truth in him. When he lies, he speaks out of his own character, for he is a liar and the father of lies. (8:42-44)

Jesus says that the devil was a murderer from the beginning. What does he mean? Way back in Genesis 4, the devil incited Cain to kill his brother Abel. One chapter earlier, in Genesis 3, the devil is shown to be the first deceiver in Scripture. He blatantly calls God a liar, telling Eve that God's command that she and her husband were not allowed to eat of the tree of the knowledge of good and evil was deceit. God said, "The day you eat of it you will surely die." The devil said to Eve, "You will surely *not* die." The devil is a murderer and a liar. It is his very character.

Why is it important for us to get that? Every lie is evidence of the effectiveness of the devil's work. Why do we lie? Because we'd rather believe the devil than what God says. The big lie was, "You've gotta look out for number one and protect your own interests. Don't listen to God. He just wants to prevent you from being in control like he's in control." Every little lie stems from that big lie.

Every murder is evidence of the effectiveness of the devil's work. Murder is more expansive than taking someone else's life. Jesus says as much in the Sermon on the Mount.

> You have heard that it was said to those of old, "You shall not murder; and whoever murders will be liable to judgment." But I say

to you that everyone who is angry with his brother will be liable to judgment; whoever insults his brother will be liable to the council; and whoever says, "You fool!" will be liable to the hell of fire. (Matthew 5:21-22)

John echoes the Lord in 1 John 3 when he writes, "We should not be like Cain, who was of the evil one and murdered his brother. . . . Everyone who hates his brother is a murderer, and you know that no murderer has eternal life abiding in him" (vv. 12, 15).

Like the Pastor, John says in 1 John 3:8, "The reason the Son of God appeared was to destroy the works of the devil." In Hebrews 2:14, the Pastor is emphasizing that Jesus has destroyed the devil through his death. Only by becoming an incarnate human being was Christ able to die, or as Hebrews 2:9 says, to "taste death for everyone." The cross of Jesus Christ was the destruction of the devil. As Jesus hung his head and died, the devil's power over death was nullified for all the children God has given him. Death was crushed to death. Satan had persuaded humanity to abandon the life God promised for death and there's no escape from the realm of death except through the one who came to destroy death.

To liberate. Jesus came not only to destroy the devil, but to liberate the slaves. In fact, his destruction of the devil was at the same time the release of slaves from bondage. Rescuing slaves was the whole point of his operation. There's a comma at the end of verse 14, not a period. He partook of flesh and blood to destroy the devil "and deliver all those who through fear of death were subject to lifelong slavery" (Hebrews 2:15).

There is a stream of theology referred to as "liberation theology," which says that the whole point of Jesus' message was freedom from political oppression, institutions, and those in positions of power who use their power to enslave others and benefit themselves. In other words, the whole point of Jesus' teaching is physical freedom—power for the powerless.

Let me try to make it practical for you. If you have a self-centered boss at work, do you believe that Jesus came to free you from that situation? If you have a teacher who plays favorites and treats students unfairly, do you believe that Jesus came to free you from having to deal with teachers like that? Do you think that Jesus came to free you from having to be under the authority of people with bad intentions? That's liberation theology. It's true up to a point, but it doesn't encompass the full liberation that the gospel is concerned with.

Yes, Jesus is a just and righteous king who is concerned with justice. We saw that in chapter one of this book when we focused on Hebrews 1:8 where the Father says to Son, "Your throne, O God, is forever and ever, the scepter of uprightness is the scepter of your kingdom." We dare not limit the liberation Christ brings in his incarnation, ministry, and resurrection to a disembodied message of spiritual freedom. Justice and righteousness reign in God's kingdom.

At the same time, no nation on earth is the kingdom of God. The slavery described in verse 15 is not physical slavery or political oppression, but lifelong slavery dominated by the fear of death. And that phrase "fear of death" is significant. He could have said that Jesus was made like us to liberate us from death, which is true. Jesus gives his people eternal life, which means they are free from death. But the Pastor says Jesus came to liberate us from the fear of death, and this has profound implications, especially when we find ourselves on the receiving end of injustice in this life.

Everyone eventually dies. We don't know when or how it's going to happen, but we know it's unavoidable. People express the fear of death in different ways. Some are petrified such that they won't go anywhere or do anything in the least bit risky. Others ignore the reality of death or avoid thinking about it by trying to make life as comfortable or as busy as possible. Some stick out their chest in defiance, taking huge risks and saying all the while, "I'm going to stare death in the face. It's not going to get the best of me." Death is not a distant reality seen only through a telescope. It rules in our minds and lives right now, permeating everything.

The Pastor is saying that Christ was made like us to free us from this fear. We may have to face intense suffering for our faith in Jesus, but we need to be reminded that there is no fear in dying for the Christian. Do you know that liberty? Or are you stuck in slavery to the fear of death, trying to avoid thinking about it, numbing yourself with pleasure and comfort instead of knowing the freedom of life in Christ?

To intercede. The reason freedom from the fear of death is not just empty words or a nice sounding idea is because of the third reason that Jesus was made like us: "Therefore, he had to be made like his brothers in every respect, so that he might become a merciful and faithful high priest in the service of God, to make propitiation for the sins of the people" (Hebrews 2:17). Jesus' death on the cross was the defeat of the devil and freedom for his brothers and sisters from the fear of death, but he didn't stay dead. He rose from the dead and is seated at the right hand of the Father. And what is he doing there? He's interceding for his people.

Jesus was made like us to intercede on our behalf as a merciful and faithful high priest in the service of God. Just because you're a Christian doesn't mean you won't have to fight hopelessness, fear, depression, anxiety, and stress. What does Jesus do when fear grips his brother's heart? What does Jesus do when his sister is overcome with anxiety? As the merciful and faithful high priest, he has the Father's ear. He says, "Father, that's my brother who's struggling with fear because his circumstances have become more important at this moment than your promises. Comfort him with your Holy Spirit. Remind him of my sacrifice and your love so that he can live by that and not by fear"; and "Father, that's my sister who's anxious over many things because her eyes are only seeing the difficulties. Comfort her with Holy Spirit. Refocus her eyes to see your glory."

He's qualified to do that because he made propitiation for the sins of the people. Literally, he wiped out the sins of the people. God put it this way through the prophet Isaiah,

> Out of the anguish of his soul he shall see and be satisfied; by his knowledge shall the righteous one, my servant, make many to be

accounted righteous, and he shall bear their iniquities. Therefore, I will divide him a portion with the many, and he shall divide the spoil with the strong, because he poured out his soul to death and was numbered with the transgressors; yet he bore the sin of many, and makes intercession for the transgressors. (Isaiah 53:11-12)

To make intercession for the transgressors—that's us—he had to be made like us in every respect. He had to be a true human if he was going to be a true priest. You and I are not nearly as concerned with sin as God is. The Pastor mentions sin with frequency. Chapter six is the only one in the whole letter of Hebrews where the word *sin* doesn't appear, though it is implied. God was determined to have worshipers. To do so he had to deal with the sins of the people. Jesus was made like us to deal with sin fully and finally, and he now makes intercession for the transgressors as our great high priest.

To help. So Jesus was made like us to destroy the devil, to liberate the slaves, to intercede as our high priest, and to help us in our temptation. "For surely it is not angels that he helps, but he helps the offspring of Abraham. . . . For because he himself has suffered when tempted, he is able to help those who are being tempted" (Hebrews 2:16, 18).

The word translated "help" literally means to be concerned with, and the sense here is being concerned to the point of taking hold of something such that it becomes your own. Jesus' concern is for those who God promised to give him. He takes a step down so that he can have our full experience. God's concern for humanity was so deep that he became human to help humanity. Because Jesus has suffered when tempted, he's able to help those who are being tempted.

The help that Jesus gives us is the strength to resist the temptation to drift away from the faith in the face of the most desperate and disappointing circumstances. What the Pastor says here is connected to what he said in Hebrews 2:1, "We must pay much closer attention to what we have heard, lest we drift away from it." Jesus resisted temptation every day of his life. He was tempted by the devil in the wilderness for forty days at the beginning of his ministry. The temptation was an easier path to glory that did not involve the cross. The Pharisees and leaders were plotting to kill him, but he resisted the temptation to call down fire from heaven to destroy them.

At every step, Jesus chose to obey his Father's will and continue walking the road of suffering so that he could help *you* as you suffer and are tempted to throw in the towel. The Pastor says, "No. Don't you understand that he went through what he went through precisely so that he could help you go through *this*?"

CONSIDER JESUS

Jesus was made like us for our benefit—to destroy the devil and liberate us from the fear of death, to wipe away our sins and make intercession as our high priest, to help us in our temptations—to bring us to glory. Faithfulness means holding onto this confession that Jesus is Lord through thick and thin, continually submitting our lives to him.

Faithfulness is on the Pastor's mind in chapter 3 when he exhorts,

> Therefore, holy brothers [and sisters], you who share in a heavenly calling, consider Jesus, the apostle and high priest of our confession, who was faithful to him who appointed him, just as Moses also was faithful in all God's house. (Hebrews 3:1-2)

Here again is another beautiful example of solid doctrine applied to life. Why consider Jesus? Why fix your thoughts on him? You might argue that's already been made clear in the first part of this chapter, but as much as has already been said about Jesus, we've only scratched the surface. There are two more ideas to emphasize at this point: one further truth about Jesus, and what it means for those who belong to Jesus.

Jesus is the faithful apostle and high priest. This is the only time in the Bible that these two terms are combined to describe Jesus. He is the apostle and high priest of our confession. But the Pastor is not communicating anything new. When he says, "Therefore," he's referring to everything he has said up to this point. Jesus is the final and complete Word of God. Jesus is the one through whom the world was created. Jesus upholds the universe by the word of his power. Jesus is worshiped by the angels. Jesus is crowned with glory and honor. Jesus is the founder of our salvation. Jesus was made perfect through suffering. Jesus is the one who sanctifies his people. Jesus destroyed the devil. Jesus helps his people when they're tempted. The Pastor has said all these things and more about Jesus in the first two chapters of Hebrews. These are core Christian beliefs about Jesus. He refers to them as "our confession."

In describing Jesus as the apostle and high priest of our confession, the Pastor is repeating himself. An apostle is one who is sent. Jesus was sent to us by the Father to proclaim God's word, to bring deliverance, to liberate his people, and bring them to glory. As high priest, he has made full atonement for sin and returned to glory to take his seat at the right hand of the Majesty on high. He intercedes for his people, and because he is both God and man, he can bring us to God and bring God's help to us.

The Pastor is repetitive because we need to hear the message over and over again. He's not concerned with the boredom of his audience. "Didn't he say that already? Can't we move on to something else?" The Pastor's response is, "Not yet." This call to consider Jesus is an invitation to respond, and it is the second exhortation in the letter. The first was in 2:1 when the Pastor said, "Therefore we must pay much closer attention to what we have heard, lest we drift away from it." Now he says, "Therefore, since you share in a heavenly calling, think on Jesus."

You will never ever get to the point where you no longer need to reflect on the Christian confession that Jesus is apostle and high priest. He's the sent one who has dealt with sin and stands as our advocate with God. Whether you're a new Christian, a longtime believer, or yet to believe in Christ at all, this is the message you need to hear. In our struggles with remaining faithful to God the solution is always to turn our attention to

Jesus. God appointed him as apostle and high priest, and he is faithful to the one who appointed him.

Jesus is the faithful builder and son. Not only is Jesus the faithful apostle and high priest, but he is also the faithful builder of God's house. In verses 2-6, the Pastor compares Jesus to Moses, building on his argument. Beginning in 1:1, he compared Jesus to the prophets of old. Then he demonstrates Jesus' superiority to angels in 1:4–2:18. Now, he holds up Jesus next to Moses. The point of these comparisons is not to denigrate the prophets or the angels or Moses, but rather it is to build up Jesus in the minds of his readers.

The Pastor has only positive things to say about Moses, and based on 3:2, you might be inclined to think that there's no difference between them. Jesus was faithful to God who appointed him just as Moses was faithful in God's house. Moses was an apostle and priest in his own right. He was sent by God to deliver God's people from slavery in Egypt so they could be free to worship God. He interceded and advocated for the people before God time and again. God says of Moses in Numbers 12:8, "With Moses I speak mouth to mouth." God's word came directly and clearly to his people through Moses, and they rightly held him in high esteem.

But the Pastor is not calling his people to fix their thoughts on Moses. He says that Jesus has been counted worthy of more glory than Moses. How so? The answer comes in the form of an image drawn from the construction industry. People travel to locations all over the world just to see famous buildings. You don't visit Egypt and only eat the food. You want to see the pyramids. When you go to Paris, you want to see the Eiffel Tower. When you go to Greece, you want to see the Parthenon. But what's even more impressive than the buildings are the brains behind them. The buildings don't get built unless they are first thought of and designed in someone's mind.

That's the comparison the Pastor is making. Jesus is worthy of more glory than Moses because he's the builder of God's house. The builder of a house has more honor than the house itself. When you look at God's house, you don't glorify Moses—you give glory to Jesus. What is this house he's talking about? It is not one made of bricks and stone. He's talking about people. He's talking about the church. The house that Jesus is building is the church.

Notice that the Pastor does not make any distinction. He does not say that Jesus has more honor than Moses because Jesus is building a new house. There has only ever been one house of God, one people of God. Jesus has always been the builder of that house. No one has ever been a member of God's house apart from faith in Christ. Whether it was the people who looked forward in faith to his promised coming or those who look back once he had come, all are part of the one house that he is building. Jesus is the faithful builder *and* Jesus is the faithful Son. Jesus is superior to Moses because the house is his design. Moses didn't come up with the idea of the house, he just worked on it.

In Hebrews 3:5-6, the Pastor directly quotes Numbers 12:7 describing Moses as the faithful servant in all God's house, but as the Son, Christ is *over* God's house. Moses *was* faithful as a servant, but Jesus *is* faithful right now as a son over God's house. Thus Jesus is worthy of more honor than anyone else.

The Pastor seemed to be in danger of putting more trust in Moses than in Jesus. Moses was worthy of honor, but he could not come close to being worthy of the honor and glory that belongs to Jesus. I doubt you are being tempted to put your trust in Moses, but there are good, honorable alternatives that we *are* tempted to trust in. God's Word exhorts us to consider Jesus, to fix our thoughts on him because the temptation is to give more honor to God's gifts than we give to God. Jesus is still building God's house (Ephesians 2:19-22; 1 Peter 2:4-5).

The Pastor writes these robust doctrinal truths about Jesus so that his readers would consider the faithfulness of Jesus. He wants them to remain faithful to their calling and endure in the faith. He wants them to realize that because these things are true about Jesus, there are certain things that are true for those who belong to him.

Notice what he calls them in Hebrews 3:1—holy brothers and sisters who share in a heavenly calling. Because of who Jesus is, if you belong to him, you are holy. That is, you are set apart by God for God. Even better, you are not left to face this life by yourself. You should not strive to be faithful to God all by yourself. To that, the Pastor says you are holy brothers and sisters. You are a family because you share in a heavenly calling. You live on earth, but your call is from heaven. You might have a job description as a parent, and employee, or a student, but if you are a Christian, your call is from heaven.

The church shares that call together. To have a heavenly calling doesn't mean a life detached from this world with your head in the clouds. To have a heavenly calling means to tune your ears to the one who speaks from heaven. This cannot be overstated. In the Christian life there is no call to part-time holiness. The heavenly call is to live in a way that demonstrates the fact that Jesus is number one.

When he says that we share in a heavenly calling, he is connecting it to Hebrews 2:14 when he declared Jesus shared in our humanity. Christ permanently connected himself to us so that we could be eternally connected to him and have ears that can hear his voice. That's why we find this conditional statement in Hebrews 3:6, "And we are his house, if indeed we hold fast our confidence and our boasting in our hope."

Christians do not walk around with their chests poked out boasting, arrogant and obnoxious. Our endurance in the faith is the evidence that we share in the heavenly calling, that we hear his voice. Faithfulness is holding firmly to our confidence, being unashamed to hope in Jesus Christ. What a phrase! "Boasting in our hope." Are we proud to hope in Christ and his promises especially through difficulty, persecution, and trial? Remember—not pride as in arrogance. Rather a forward-facing, humble posture that always considers Jesus when in the danger zone.

3

RESTING IN THE DANGER ZONE

We can rest knowing the Lord's presence transcends
what we feel. Just like the flow of the air, he is moving
even if his movements cannot be perceived. And where
God is not just felt but known, faith and confidence grow.
Affliction is a swindler, so we must guard resolutely our
conviction that God is present and that in Christ we overcome.

ALICIA AKINS, *INVITATIONS TO ABUNDANCE*

I have two sweet granddaughters. They're just under thirteen months apart and both are still infants. I'm discovering that grandparent life is the best life there is. I would move heaven and earth for my children, and that commitment increases exponentially with grandchildren. There's nothing like it! But as sweet and precious as they are, my granddaughters have a problem. They don't like to share.

The eldest had her home and parents to herself for a full year, and we wondered what her reaction would be upon meeting her new sister. My son and daughter-in-law prepared her for her sister's arrival throughout the pregnancy. "¿Dónde está Fifi (short for fetus)?" they would ask. Over time she would tap my daughter-in-law's belly in response. When they met for the first time, the elder looked strangely at the younger. All was well until they gave the newborn a pacifier. That was a step too far. It didn't matter that the eldest had three pacifiers of her own. Anything that looked like a pacifier belonged to her. She reached for her new sister's pacifier, but she wasn't allowed to take it, which left her very unhappy. Tears ensued.

We teach children all kinds of words, but *mine* is one they seem to pick up all by themselves. It's like their little brains prioritize being able to clearly communicate when something belongs to them. Sometimes it doesn't even have to belong to a child for them to claim it. All they have to do is want it. So parents continually find themselves saying, "No, honey, that doesn't belong to you."

Thankfully, it only has to be said once and then you never have that problem again, right? Once you tell them to share their stuff, all vestiges of selfishness and self-centeredness vanish, never to appear again. Isn't that what happened when your parents told you the same?

Of course not. Both of my granddaughters will learn and relearn the lesson of what it means to love others as we love ourselves for the remainder of their days. There is one, however, who can justifiably be self-centered in a crucial way. God is the only one who doesn't have to share. He says in Isaiah 42:8, "I am the LORD; that is my name; my glory I give to no other, nor my praise to carved idols." And again, in Isaiah 48:11, he says, "My glory I will not give to another."

The heavens declare God's glory (Psalm 19:1). The whole earth is full of his glory (Isaiah 6:3). God's Spirit is the Spirit of glory (1 Peter 4:14). And as we've already seen, Jesus is the radiance of God's glory (Hebrews 1:3). Our triune God is completely justified in refusing to share his glory with anyone else. His self-centeredness is not a problem. Rather, it is a blessing for us. There is a day coming when every knee will bow, and every tongue will confess that Jesus is Lord to the glory of God the Father (Philippians 2:10-11). The blessing for us is the ability to rest as we hope for the coming of that day.

God, who does not have to share anything, least of all with sinners, has promised to share his rest with everyone who trusts in him. Faith in Jesus

Christ means rest, but not any old rest—a particular rest that everyone needs. It means sharing in *God's rest*. Gospel hope is not a hustler, but as my friend Alicia Akins says, "Affliction is a swindler."[1] Afflictions threaten our joy and peace. They shake our faith, and they can deprive us of rest.

In Hebrews 3:7–4:13 the Pastor's overriding concern is that his people would not miss out on the promise to enter God's rest. When he says, "While the promise of entering his rest still stands" (4:1), the English word *entering* is two words in Greek in order to emphasize the action. A word-for-word translation would be, "While the promise of *entering into* his rest still stands." The word *enter* appears eleven times in this section, and in nine of those times the Pastor is saying, "Enter into."

Why point that out? Because what he's doing here is something that he does throughout this letter. He continues to direct the eyes of his readers forward and upward to the heavenly reality so they can endure and thrive in the here and now as they journey toward heaven. He wants to drive home the heavenly reality as the most important thing to grasp.

They are no different than we are. People haven't changed that much. What dominates our lives and thoughts are the circumstances we face every day. We are most passionate about those things. Grasping the heavenly reality is the opposite of having our minds up in the clouds somewhere, daydreaming, ignoring the issues we face, pretending they don't exist. The Pastor knows their hardships are real, but there is something more real than their hardships. This world is not going to remain jacked up forever. A time is coming when all the mess is going to be done away with (Hebrews 12:26-27), and those who trust in Jesus Christ will enter his rest.

The Pastor's concern over their being swindled by their afflictions is so serious that in Hebrews 4:1-3 he includes both the warning about missing God's rest and the promise of entering God's rest.

Therefore, while the promise of entering his rest still stands, let us fear lest any of you should seem to have failed to reach it. For good news came to us just as to them, but the message they heard did not benefit them, because they were not united by faith with those who listened. For we who have believed enter that rest, as he has said, "As I swore in my wrath, 'They shall not enter my rest,'" although his works were finished from the foundation of the world.

The first word in verse 1 of the Greek text is what is translated "let us fear." Since the generation that Moses led out of Egypt was unable to enter God's rest because of unbelief, *let us fear* that none of you should seem to have failed to reach it while the promise to enter his rest still stands.

Notice that this is a collective fearing. The Pastor doesn't say, "Y'all be afraid." He's including himself in the warning. Let *us* fear. It is a collective, corporate holy fear and concern that some members of the church will fall off and fail to obtain God's promised rest because of unbelief. The fear he prescribes is not that of hiding under the covers, paralyzed with fright. Rather, it is a fear that leads to striving, specifically in what the Pastor calls them to in verse 11: "Let us therefore strive to enter that rest."

It is critical to understand this fear as a united concern about every person in the church, one tied to the instruction in 3:13, "Exhort one another every day, as long as it is called 'today,' that none of you may be hardened by the deceitfulness of sin." For a church to be heathy, there must be a healthy care and concern for the needs of every person. Galatians 6 tells us to "bear one another's burdens" and "do good to everyone, especially those who are of the household of faith."

In the context of what the Pastor says here, this fear is a holy concern for every person to believe the gospel as the community endures affliction. Doing so ensures that "swindler" will fail in convincing people they have believed a lie. The Bible knows nothing of the exaltation of individualism. I have rights and protections as an individual under the law, but individualism says I define my own self. I don't have any natural interests extending beyond myself. I don't have any prescribed duties to anyone unless it benefits me.

God has promised to give rest to his people and he wants us to have such care, love, and concern for one another that we're not content with anyone failing to reach it because they never really believed the gospel. The Pastor says in 4:2, "Good news came to us just as to them, but the message they heard didn't benefit them, because they were not united by faith with those who listened." He is reminding them that their forefathers and foremothers who were delivered from slavery in Egypt also had the gospel. But they demonstrated their lack of faith through an ongoing unbelief and disobedience in the face of suffering.

A CAPACITY FOR ENDURING SUFFERING

During the height of the pandemic, when every community event was virtual, my friend Dr. Greg Thompson led a three-part lecture series for our church titled, "Love in the Streets: The Faith-Based Civil Rights Movement and the Contemporary Church." The focus of his second lecture was on the essential work of Rev. James Lawson. Among other important things, Rev. Lawson provided biblical, theological, and ethical training for young people like John Lewis, Diane Nash, and countless others that prepared them for the nonviolent social action of the sit-in movement. Rev. Lawson told Dr. Thompson that by the time he met Martin Luther King Jr., he had already spent ten years researching, reading, and studying pacifism and New Testament social ethics.

What he desired to accomplish in his training was to provide people with the formative foundations necessary to be a people of love. Indeed, the civil rights movement itself was based in the Christian ethic of love, which determined both its means and desired ends. Dr. Thompson said, "The desire was to bring about social change that enabled social healing on the other side."[2] The participants of the sit-ins endured incredible suffering and ridicule through their nonviolent social action.

The cost of their action was on bold relief for me in the fall of 2022 when I partnered with a colleague to lead a walking tour of the Nashville sit-ins. It was part of a training regimen we were providing to a Christian organization and because it took place in Nashville, the tour was a perfect opportunity to see firsthand the boldness often required to be a prophetic voice for God in the culture. John Lewis and Diane Nash, both Fisk University students, were among the leaders of the Nashville sit-ins that began in February 1960. The lunch counter at Woolworth's was the site of three protests in 1960: February 13, 27, and April 11.

The February 27 protest was the most violent, resulting in several arrests, including the first of fifty for Congressman John Lewis. Despite being dressed in their Sunday best and sitting respectfully, they were subjected to verbal and physical abuse for breaking unjust laws and customs. How were they able to endure? They were formed to love their enemies by Rev. Lawson.

During his series at our church, Dr. Thompson laid out the five foundations of Rev. Lawson's "School of Love" that formed people for the work of social change that enables social healing on the other side. Foundational principle number four was "a capacity for enduring suffering," a principle that appears often throughout the pages of the New Testament.

Jesus told his disciples, "A disciple is not above his teacher, nor a servant above his master. It is enough for the disciple to be like his teacher, and the servant like his master. If they have called the master of the house Beelzebul, how much more will they malign those of his household" (Matthew 10:24-25). Christians are united to Jesus Christ by faith. His love is demonstrated in his unjust suffering for the redemption of the world. When Christians suffer unjustly, we bear witness to our redeemer's power (1 Peter 2:20-21).

Jesus goes so far as to declare that those who suffer for righteousness' sake are blessed. The kingdom of heaven belongs to them (Matthew 5:10). The servant not being above his master is not just a biblical aphorism to which we give mental ascent. This aspect of Christian servanthood is an ethical fact. In his lecture, Dr. Thompson asked, "Because Jesus is the one who loves through suffering, how can we imagine a life of faith that is different than that?"[3] The violence of this world will land on shoulders of

God's people as they seek to be faithful to him. Jesus learned obedience to God through what he suffered (Hebrews 5:8, more on that in the next chapter). So it is with those who follow him.

How do you build a capacity for enduring suffering by faith? Lean into what it means to share in God's rest with the community of believers. There is a throughline between enduring by faith, being formed for love, and sharing in God's rest.

DESCRIBING GOD'S REST

The Pastor has been talking about God's rest since 3:7, but he hasn't really described what God's rest is like. Now, in 4:3-5, he provides insight into God's rest: "For he has somewhere spoken of the seventh day in this way: 'And God rested on the seventh day from all his works'" (v. 4). God's works were finished from the foundation of the world, according to Genesis 2:2. God has been resting since the seventh day of creation.

In a very real sense, God's rest is the goal of creation. When you read the creation account in Genesis 1:1–2:3, you will see that each day ends with the statement "There was evening and there was morning." There was evening and there was morning, the first day, the second day, the third day, all the way to the sixth day. But on the seventh day, there is no evening to conclude it and no morning to begin an eighth day.

God's rest is already and has been a reality since the creation of the world. It's a future reality only in relation to the rest promised to his people who have yet to enter it. If God has been resting since the creation of the world, we have to ask, In what way is he resting? Did he stop working? Was he tired? Was he weary from all that creating?

When Jesus was persecuted by the Jewish leaders for healing on the Sabbath, he said to them in John 5:17, "My Father is working until now, and I am working." Psalm 121 declares that the Lord neither slumbers nor sleeps. Isaiah tells us that the Lord is the everlasting God, the Creator of the ends of the earth, and he does not faint or grow weary (Isaiah 40:28).

The Lord rested on the seventh because his labors were *finished*. His work was done. He rested on the seventh day in the sense of celebrating the completion of his work. He looked over all that he had made and saw that it was very good. Exodus 31:17 puts it this way, "In six days the LORD made heaven and earth, and on the seventh day he rested and was refreshed." His resting and refreshment are an ongoing rejoicing in his finished work. God's rest is not inactivity, idleness, or a ceasing of all work. He's still working. He's still fulfilling his plans for this world. But his work is like work that's not work.

Have you ever had a job that was a perfect fit? A job that was a joy to go to, that you looked forward to every day? A job that didn't leave you tired but refreshed? Does that sound too good to be true? Well, just imagine it, and then multiply it by infinity and you might begin to have an idea of what God's rest is like. It's work without labor. It's activity that coincides with resting and enjoying.

URGENTLY RESPONDING TO GOD'S REST

Immediately after this brief description of God's rest the Pastor turns to the urgent need of responding to God's rest.

> Since therefore it remains for some to enter it, and those who formerly received the good news failed to enter because of disobedience, again he appoints a certain day, "Today," saying through David so long afterward, in the words already quoted, "Today, if you hear his voice, do not harden your hearts." (4:6-7)

Since it remains for some to enter God's rest, God appoints a certain day and calls it "Today." And what does God say today? If you hear his voice, do not harden your hearts. Today won't last forever, but for now, it's still "Today." As P. Hughes says,

> In the language of Psalm 95, it is still "today" as far as God's promise is concerned; and this indicates both opportunity and responsibility: opportunity in that we live in God's day of grace,

and responsibility on our part not to despise or turn away from this privilege.[4]

This is the fourth time in this section that the Pastor has either said or implied, "Today, if you hear his voice, do not harden your hearts." The call is urgent and immediate. It's a call to respond to the gospel, described here as the promise to enter into God's rest.

The time to check our response to that promise is today, not tomorrow. Remember, he's writing to the church, telling them to check their hearts to see if they are hardened by the deceitfulness of sin. It is important to point out the life circumstance of the Exodus generation who failed to enter God's rest. They were in the wilderness, facing uncertainty and enemies, both very real threats to God's promise. In the face of this opposition, they put God to the test instead of responding to the test of their faith with confidence. "We were like grasshoppers" compared to the inhabitants of the Promised Land is the report the spies brought back to the people (Numbers 13:33). The people grumbled against Moses and Aaron and rejected God. "Let's choose a leader and go back to Egypt," they said (Numbers 14:4).

The Pastor's connects this historical event to his present point to emphasize it is not just a story about the past. The threat that the wilderness experience presents to God's people is always current. The warning is as applicable in the twenty-first century as it was to those who first heard the words of Psalm 95.

SHARING GOD'S REST

The reality that God's promised rest is still out there is reinforced in verse 8 when the Pastor says, "For if Joshua had given them rest, God would not have spoken of another day later on." When Joshua led the people into the Promised Land, conquering the land of Canaan, that wasn't the final rest God was talking about. God's rest is not about a plot of land or securing some material possession we think can satisfy us. The rest that God promises to share with his people is far better.

In verse 9, the Pastor calls it a "Sabbath rest." The phrase derives from a single word and this is the only time it appears in the New Testament. More importantly, it does not refer to a single day. What is this Sabbath rest like? It is nothing short of God sharing *his* rest with his people. The Pastor says, "Whoever enters God's rest rests from his labors just like God did from his own" (Hebrews 4:10, author's translation). In this Sabbath rest, just like the seventh day of creation, there is no end.

I used to tease my kids on Sunday night about the joy of going back to school on Monday morning. They would contort their faces and look at me with displeasure. In the Sabbath rest, there are no more Monday morning blues. The Mighty Clouds of Joy put it well in their gospel song "Walk Around Heaven" when they sang, "Everyday will be Sunday, my Lord. Sabbath will have no end." The Pastor is describing an everlasting rest. While there's still work, the Sabbath rest is a celebration of the rest God shares with us, which is rest from labor and toil and hardship. It's full of joy and feasting. It's a delight, not a drag. It's a time of abundance, rather than scarcity.

This rest is paradoxically a present and future reality. "Whoever has entered God's rest has also rested from his works as God did from his" (Hebrews 4:10). It is true rest right now through Jesus, our great high priest (Hebrews 4:14). A primary way that we experience sharing in God's rest is through corporate worship on the Lord's Day. God gives us a taste of his promised Sabbath rest every week.

Each Sunday, our worship is a taste of heaven. We experience a glimpse of what it will be when the curse is removed. As we gather for worship, sing God's praise, offer up our prayers, hear his Word, and rejoice in the salvation that Jesus Christ has purchased for us, we participate in a dress rehearsal for the promised Sabbath rest. That's why the Pastor will say to the church in 12:22,

> But you have come to Mount Zion and to the city of the living God, the heavenly Jerusalem, and to innumerable angels in festal gathering, and to the assembly of the firstborn who are enrolled in

heaven, and to God, the judge of all, and to the spirits of the righteous made perfect, and to Jesus, the mediator of a new covenant, and to the sprinkled blood that speaks a better word than the blood of Abel.

When the church gathers for worship, we are brought up by the Spirit of God to the heavenly Jerusalem to innumerable angels, to the entire assembly, to the entire church, to everyone enrolled in heaven in festal gathering. We come to God the Father and God the Son through God the Spirit. Every Sunday we share God's rest. What he did, we do. By our identification with him, we enter his experience of rest. We get a weekly foretaste now to help carry us to the day when Sabbath rest will not have to be experienced by faith because it will be lived by sight. This makes the church's worship an indispensable part of Christian hope.

The corporate nature of Christian hope is further emphasized by the exhortation in verse 11, "Let us therefore strive to enter that rest, so that no one may fall by the same sort of disobedience." And just like 4:1 was a corporate call ("Let *us* fear") so it is here when he says, "Let *us* strive." We strive to enter God's rest so that no one falls by the same pattern of disobedience that Israel displayed in the wilderness. We strive together because we don't want to see anyone left out.

Back in 2:13, the Pastor put the words of Isaiah 8:17 on the lips of Jesus speaking to the Father, "I myself will trust in him" (author's translation). What we find in 4:11 is the negation of that word "trust" found in 2:13. So Jesus says, "I'm leading my people in a life of worship. They worship me. They worship my Father. As I unreservedly put my trust in my Father, so also my people will trust him without reservation." But the disobedient heart says, "I will *not* trust." And the Pastor says, "If that's the way you want it, you will fall. There's no other option." The guaranteed outcome of not trusting is failing to enter God's promised rest. So strive together, he says, make every effort to enter God's rest. He presses this so strongly because he knows that it is the greatest blessing imaginable for those who believe in God through faith in Jesus Christ. Alternatively, eternal separation from God's rest is the worst fate imaginable for those who don't trust in God through faith in Jesus Christ.

Have you ever considered the fact that hell can be described this way—as eternal separation from God's rest? Take your worst workday where all you want to do is get out of there and go home and rest. Take that feeling and multiply it exponentially. Students: imagine the stress you feel when you have a huge test coming up that you're not prepared for and all you want is for the test to be over. That stress and anxiety can move people to tears. Hold that feeling and imagine it intensified a million times. Then imagine that being the state of your existence forever. It's the type of stress and anxiety that results in heart attacks. But these heart attacks don't kill. They continue without end, creating that same terrible state forever. That's hell.

We don't like to talk about the consequences of unbelief because they make us uncomfortable, but the Pastor knows they're real. As sobering as this is, he's not presenting God as a mean ogre waiting to lay the hammer on you for disobedience. The very next paragraph (vv. 14-16) calls us to draw near to God's throne. And he doesn't call it the throne of judgment. Rather, he calls it the throne of grace because we have a great high priest in Jesus who has made it possible for us to receive mercy and find grace to help in our time of need. The warning in 4:11 is intended to point us to Jesus. Make every effort to enter God's rest, not by trying to earn it, but by holding firmly to our confidence in Christ.

It's no coincidence then that the Pastor moves from urging his readers to make every effort to enter God's rest directly into talking about the power of God's Word. How are they going to avoid falling by the same pattern of disobedience? By exposing their hearts to God's Word and responding in repentance and faith. From beginning to end, the Bible testifies self-referentially to its own power and authority.[5] The Pastor is doing the same thing in Hebrews 4:12 as an encouragement to continue striving for God's rest through his Word, "For the word of God is living and active, sharper than any two-edged sword, piercing to the division of soul and of spirit, of joints and of marrow, and discerning the thoughts and intentions of the heart." The Word of God is alive. Because it's alive, it naturally follows that it is active, specifically in the sense of being effective. A pastor preaches God's Word, but the pastor doesn't make it effective. The effectiveness of God's Word is not based on how eloquently it's shared, but by virtue of what it is.

Its effectiveness is also displayed by its sharpness. The Word pierces, penetrating to the division of soul, spirit, joints, and marrow. It cuts right through whatever fluff you try to put up. The way we try to present ourselves to other people doesn't work with God. His Word confronts us to the core. Therefore, the Word of God discerns the thoughts, or deliberations, and intentions of your heart. I use the word *deliberations* intentionally here. It's a valid alternative translation, and I prefer it in this context because the Pastor's audience is dealing with temptations to sin. They are facing temptations to act in ways that demonstrate unbelief. And the Pastor is trying to show them that these deliberations are taking place inside their hearts. *Should I or shouldn't I? Will I or won't I?* God's Word exposes them for what they are. The Word of God lays bare the true intentions of our hearts.

We are experts at fooling ourselves. That's why the Pastor includes his exhortation in 3:13 to keep from being hardened by the deceitfulness of sin. We can head down the road of self-deceit, but God's Word won't let us off the hook. It penetrates to the very core of our being. The question for us today is this: What deliberations are God's Word revealing to us that need to change? God's Word is sharper than any double-edged sword. It's going to penetrate. It's going to pierce. And when it does, one of two things will happen: you'll either respond in repentance and faith, turning to God for grace, mercy, and help, or your heart will harden, and you'll grow angry with God and reject his Word. You'll pick and choose what you like and reject what you don't.

We strive for God's rest in this life by means of God's powerful, effective, penetrating Word. This is the Word that tells us God will not give his glory to another. Indeed, I began this chapter with the claim that God will not share his glory, but he has promised to share his rest. Why is this relevant for our time? Because it's always "today." The things that are wrong in our lives and in our world are swindlers, intent on leading us into unbelief. The most faithful Christian communities are those who form their members, not for a life of comfort and affluence, but for a life of witness that is willing to bear up under affliction. We are tempted to believe that the most appropriate and satisfactory response to the violence and suffering we endure is more violence. But this is false. The most satisfactory response is to lean into sharing God's rest.

There is, however, another way of understanding the promise of sharing God's rest. To share in God's rest *is* to share in his glory. This flows from being united to Jesus Christ by faith. In John 17, Jesus offers up his high priestly prayer prior to his crucifixion and says,

> I do not ask for these only, but also for those who will believe in me through their word, that they may all be one, just as you, Father, are in me, and I in you, that they also may be in us, so that the world may believe that you have sent me. The glory that you have given me I have given to them, that they may be one even as we are one, I in them and you in me, that they may become perfectly one, so that the world may know that you sent me and loved them even as you loved me. Father, I desire that they also, whom you have given me, may be with me where I am, to see my glory that you have given me because you loved me before the foundation of the world. (vv. 20-24)

On his heart are all believers. The glory of our triune God is on display here as the Son petitions the Father for the unity of his people. That unity can only be accomplished through the work of the Spirit who leads us into all truth.

Do you hear the notes of Christian unity flowing from union with God as our Savior says, "That they may also be in us"? What does Jesus do when we are in him? He shares his glory! Why? For our unity! When the Pastor exhorts his readers to strive for holiness and peace with everyone, not allowing the defilement of bitterness to take root among them (Hebrews 12:14-15), the basis for that exhortation is that God disciplines his people that they might share his holiness (Hebrews 12:10). God is a gracious giver!

We looked at Jesus' joining himself to us in his incarnation. From that point into his high priesthood and eternity, he is joined to us forever. As Hendrickson and Kistemaker write, "The glory which Jesus gives to believers means that they have become one plant with him; that *he* cannot be conceived of apart from *them*."[6] Jesus was not joking when he said, "Come to me, all who labor and are heavy laden, and I will give you rest" (Matthew 11:28). To know Jesus is to be brought into his glory and share in his rest. Jesus' trust in his Father is so unshakable that he can sleep in the stern of a boat while waves are crashing and a storm is raging (Matthew 8:24; Mark 4:38; Luke 8:23). This is what his rest looks like.

We grow weary of asking, "How long, O Lord?" We want God to "rend the heavens and come down" (Isaiah 64:1) to bring shalom. In the silence and the waiting, we can harden our hearts. In response to that temptation, Scripture exhorts us to rest as we wait. We practically demonstrate our ability to rest when we hope in God's power, control, and purpose despite evidence to the contrary.

PART 2

KEEP HOPE ALIVE

4

THE UNREASONABLE HOPE

You must never stop dreaming. Face reality, yes, but don't stop
with the way things are. Dream of things as they ought to be.
Dream. Face pain, but love, hope faith and dreams will help you
rise above the pain. Use hope and imagination as weapons of
survival and progress, but you keep on dreaming, young America.

REV. JESSE JACKSON, 1988 DEMOCRATIC
NATIONAL CONVENTION ADDRESS

In 1988 Rev. Jesse Jackson ran an unsuccessful campaign to become the
Democratic nominee for the presidential election. I remember when he
made his campaign stop in New York City. I was a nineteen-year-old
college student at the time. I went with some of my friends to a campaign
rally at a hotel in Manhattan to hear his speech. It was electric, but what's
funny is that now, over thirty years later, I don't remember anything he
said. My only memory is the end of his speech when he said, "Keep
hope alive!"

He brought down the house at that rally, and he did the same that
summer at the Democratic National Convention. In a sermonic way, displaying his Black church roots, he had the crowd on their feet in response
to his final exhortation, "Keep hope alive! Keep hope alive! Keep hope

alive!" At the time, I was caught up in the emotion of the moment, but later I remember asking myself—hope in what? I think the hope Rev. Jackson referred to was that those who were oppressed, impoverished, lacking education, and struggling to meet the necessities of life could still hope in the American dream. They could still hold on to the belief that this country would provide opportunity to overcome their circumstances. During his 1988 DNC speech he said, "But you keep on dreaming, young America." Face the present reality but use hope as a weapon of survival and progress. Twenty years later, in 2008, many in America saw the election of Barack Obama as at least a partial fulfillment of that hope.

Hope, however, is a tricky thing. Everybody is hoping for something. In Rev. Jackson's case, the hope was for justice, equality, and opportunity. But hope *for* something has got to be based *on* something if it is to be valid. I need a reason to be hopeful or I'm just wasting my time. What was the basis for Rev. Jackson's hope? You might say it was the Constitution. If the Constitution were to be followed, then hope for justice and opportunity was valid for everyone in the country, regardless of race or class. But hope is tricky. Even if the Constitution is the basis for your hope, you're still dependent on *people* to adhere to it for your hope to become reality. And as we know, people are unreliable. This actually makes holding on to hope seem unreasonable.

The key word there is *seem*. I wouldn't have written this book if I believed hope was unreasonable. Valid hope is based on the promises of God. And hoping in the promises of God is a hope that cannot disappoint because *that* hope is validated by God himself. It is not conditioned on the decisions of people at all. The Rev. Jesse Jackson was not the first to say, "Keep hope alive!" The Pastor wrote it to the Hebrews too.

UNREASONABLE HOPE

In Hebrews 3, the Pastor said that while Moses was faithful in God's house as a servant, Christ is faithful over God's house as a Son. In Hebrews 5:1-6, he makes a comparison between Aaron and Christ as high

priests. Where Aaron and his descendants were high priests who identified with the people because they shared in their sin, Christ is a high
priest of a different magnitude. He's greater because he can identify with
the people through suffering but without sin.

He's a priest after the order of Melchizedek, an ancient figure mentioned only two times in the Old Testament (Genesis 14:18; Psalm 110:4).
In Genesis 14, Melchizedek is called priest of God Most High and pro-
nounces a blessing on Abraham. He appears in the Bible as a priest
without any reference to a beginning or an end. The point of the comparison here in Hebrews is that Christ is like that. He is the eternal Son
of God. He never had a beginning, and he doesn't have an ending. And
because the Father designated him to be a High Priest, he embraced
human weakness.

How do we know that?

In the days of his flesh, Jesus offered up prayers and supplications,
with loud cries and tears, to him who was able to save him from
death, and he was heard because of his reverence. Although he was
a son, he learned obedience through what he suffered. And being
made perfect, he became the source of eternal salvation to all who
obey him, being designated by God a high priest after the order of
Melchizedek. (Hebrews 5:7-10)

In the days of his flesh, that is, in the days of his life here on earth, Jesus
was characterized by living a life of prayer. And the Pastor's description
of his prayer life is vivid. To make supplication is almost to beg. It has
that type of humility associated with it. Jesus' prayers were not meek,
quiet, or soft. Rather, they were offered up with loud, or strong, cries
with tears. We may naturally assume the Pastor is referring to Jesus' prayer
in the Garden of Gethsemane on the night before his arrest and crucifixion. But the Pastor doesn't say Jesus offered up one prayer on one day
with loud cries and tears. In the days of his flesh, Jesus offered up *prayers*
and *supplications*.

What's being described is the paradox of perfect human weakness unmixed with sin. Jesus had a kind of weakness that was unassociated with sin. What do I mean? Jesus was born in a manger. He needed protection. He needed nurturing. He needed to be provided for. So his weakness related to the limitations of what it means to be human, which is made more pronounced when compared to his all-powerful and unlimited divine nature.

That's how Jesus could tell his disciples when they asked him about his return, "Concerning that day and hour no one knows, not even the angels of heaven, nor the Son, but the Father only" (Matthew 24:36). In his humanity, he didn't know everything. The Pastor says that he learned obedience through the things he suffered. Even though he was a Son, even though he was without sin, throughout his life he grew in his understanding of what it meant to obey God in everything. Every challenge, every temptation to turn away from his mission, every accusation and attack was met with obedience. As R. B. Jamieson points out, the Pastor knows he's uttering a paradox when he says that the divine Son learned obedience through suffering.[1]

Don't be fooled into thinking it was easy for Jesus. The point of talking about his prayers and supplications as being made "with strong cries and tears" is so that we're not deceived into thinking that Jesus' sufferings were no problem for him. He knew his human weakness needed to be countered by his Father's strength. And he was desperate for it. He knew his Father was able to save him from death—not from dying. That "from" in verse 7 means "out of." He knew his physical death would not be the end. His Father was able to deliver him back to life. So, he pressed his Father for strength, and because he prayed like that, displaying his reverent dependence on his Father, he was heard. The fact that our weakness is still linked to sin means that we need someone whose weakness wasn't linked to sin.

We would much prefer to have hope from a position of strength than from weakness and limits. Part of the issue with our failing to remain hopeful is an unwillingness to embrace our limits and our weaknesses as good gifts. This is not to say that sin is a blessing, but it is to say that because of our finitude we will always have limits in how righteous, all-encompassing, and capable our individual selves, systems, structures, and institutions are in bringing about the fullness of shalom.

WE NEED A LION

My ministry work requires a significant amount of travel. One of its benefits is compiling lots of rewards miles from airlines. Sometimes I will use them to upgrade my seat to first class, especially when I'm tired and want to lean into the introvert side of my personality. That was my plan on a trip to Florida during the fall of 2019. As you might imagine, I'm telling you this story because things did not go according to plan!

I took my seat and proceeded to put on my over-the-ear headphones to indicate to others I wanted to be left alone. The gentleman sitting next to me ignored my cue. "I'm John," he said as he reached out to shake my hand. I slipped one side of the headphones off my ear and said, "I'm Irwyn. Nice to meet you." I still had hope of disengaging, but he asked a follow up question. "What do you do?" Internal dread came over me, expecting that my answer was going to set up further conversation. "I'm a pastor." "Oh," he said, "I'm a minister too!" This led to an extended conversation from DC to Florida.

John was returning home from a visit to the White House for a round-table discussion between several evangelical leaders and President Donald J. Trump. John was a big fan of President Trump. I was not. He sang the president's praises to me regarding policies he believed were being implemented that made life better for Christians in the United States. I asked whether he had any concerns about the president's moral life and behavior. He responded, "We need a lion in the White House! It's no coincidence that Donald Trump is the forty-fifth president. In Isaiah 45, God calls Cyrus his anointed. God can use anyone to bless his people!" Of course, the last part of John's response is true. The first part is biblical gymnastics and utterly ridiculous.

The primary emphasis of John's argument was the need for Christians to have a seat at the table, a position of influence in the halls of power to protect our interests. My primary emphasis was the regular message of Scripture that Christians bear witness to the power of God through our weakness. I would point to the examples in the Scriptures, particularly the Sermon on the Mount, where the expectation was that following the Lord would mean persecution (and blessing), and that the response was not a grab for political power. Those points were less important to him than viewing the president as "God's anointed."

Christians live a cross-bearing life as we follow our Lord, demonstrating our need for his strength. The risen and ascended Christ tells the apostle Paul in 2 Corinthians 12:9, "My grace is sufficient for you, for my power is made perfect in weakness." Paul's response to that message was,

> Therefore I will boast all the more gladly of my weaknesses, so that the power of Christ may rest upon me. For the sake of Christ, then, I am content with weaknesses, insults, hardships, persecutions, and calamities. For when I am weak, then I am strong. (2 Corinthians 12:9-10)

That is not the language of striving for the halls of civic power to maintain self-protection. We do, as Charles Taylor writes, live in a secular age.[2] Along with our secular age is a philosophical commitment to the primacy of the individual. David Koyzis is correct in his assertion, "An emphasis on rights without counteremphasis on responsibilities leaves us with precious little basis for genuine community, as we North Americans are learning to our great regret."[3] The "secularness" of the age leaves many Christians uneasy and clamoring for a return to the days of more agency in determining cultural priorities.

Political polarization in the United States and the church threatens Christian hope by diluting our witness. It is a detriment to the witness of Christ's church when we are beholden to a political party. Our witness to the reconciling power of God in Jesus Christ is damaged when our congregations are known for being either red or blue. Yes, indeed, the Spirit of Christ brings Republicans, Democrats, and Independents together in the same body, eager to maintain the unity of the Spirit in the bond of peace (Ephesians 4:3)!

The importance of my multi-hour conversation with John was not to make a case one way or the other about how Christians ought to engage appropriately in politics and with politicians. It was about strength and weakness. Jesus, while we were still weak, died for us (Romans 5:6). And the call to embrace the reality of our weakness takes a particular shape in civic life. It looks like bearing reproach for the sake of others. This is the difference between what John and others were after in their meeting with the president and what took place during the civil rights movement's "School of Love" in the previous chapter. That movement was on behalf of the oppressed, the disinherited, the disenfranchised, all of whom were on the receiving end of systemic injustice. It was not a self-seeking attempt to maintain power and influence.

Christian hope is unreasonable because we are forced to embrace our weakness and limits as a primary way of living. Hoping in God requires faith and patience because it is unreasonable to our natural minds. He takes too long for our tastes. He doesn't respond the way we want him to respond when we want him to respond. God does not operate on our agenda. We have to operate on his.

The Pastor understands the unreasonableness of our hope, which is why he introduces Abraham as an example in Hebrews 6:13-15, "For when God made a promise to Abraham, since he had no one greater by whom to swear, he swore by himself, saying, 'Surely I will bless you and multiply you.' And thus Abraham, having patiently waited, obtained the promise." God first made a promise to Abraham in Genesis 12 upon telling him to leave his father's house in Ur of the Chaldeans and go to a land God would show him. He promised to make Abraham a great nation and bless him and make his name great. Even more, God promised that all of the families of the earth would be blessed through Abraham. But there was a problem. Abraham and his wife, Sarah, had no children because she was barren.

That's why the Lord made another promise to Abraham in Genesis 15, right after Abraham was blessed by Melchizedek. He declared that the patriarch's own son would be his heir, and miracle of miracles, Isaac was born to Sarah in Genesis 21. The son of promise arrived. Now, if you're familiar with the Old Testament, you know what's coming next. Only one chapter after this miraculous birth, the Lord says to Abraham, "Take your son, your only son Isaac, whom you love, and go to the land of Moriah, and offer him there as a burnt offering on one of the mountains of which I shall tell you." So the Lord miraculously delivers on his promise to provide an heir to Abraham and then tells him to sacrifice his son. Can you imagine yourself in that situation?

Yet, this is why the Pastor introduces Abraham as an example of the unreasonableness of hope. Rather than despair or look for ways to avoid God's command, Abraham responded in faith and obedience. Here's how the Pastor describes his disposition,

> By faith Abraham, when he was tested, offered up Isaac, and he who had received the promises was in the act of offering up his only son, of whom it was said, "Through Isaac shall your offspring be named." He considered that God was able even to raise him from the dead, from which, figuratively speaking, he did receive him back. (Hebrews 11:17-19)

The apostle Paul says in Romans 4:18 that in hope Abraham believed against hope that he should become the father of many nations. Why would Abraham have to believe against hope? Because apart from faith it is unreasonable to hope in God. So, the Pastor says in Hebrews 6:15, "and thus" or "in this way," Abraham, having patiently waited, obtained the promise. In what way? In the way of faith! By faith and patience, Abraham obtained the promise that God would bless him and multiply him.

The unreasonable but sure hope of the gospel is that we enter the kingdom of God through many tribulations (Acts 14:22). That's what the Pastor's readers are experiencing, which is why he directs their gaze to

Abraham to point out that his hope may have seemed unreasonable, but Abraham obtained the promise because this unreasonable hope is a valid hope.

VALID HOPE

What makes this hope valid? According to the Pastor, it is because God swore on himself when making his promise to Abraham. There was no one greater by whom to swear. Then he says, "For people swear by something greater than themselves, and in all their disputes an oath is final for confirmation. So when God desired to show more convincingly to the heirs of the promise the unchangeable character of his purpose, he guaranteed it with an oath" (6:16-17). In the ancient world, oaths were the substance of legal contracts. You would confirm the oath by swearing on something greater than yourself. Repeatedly in the Old Testament we see the phrase "as the Lord lives" when people make a promise.

Such phrasing is not far removed from our modern conventions before testifying in court. Every witness is asked, "Do you solemnly swear to tell the truth, the whole truth, and nothing but the truth, so help you God?" To testify, you must swear by something greater than yourself. You've got to take an oath, and it is taken seriously. Lying under oath is a crime in the American court system that can result in jail time. So when the Pastor says that the oath is the final proof for settling any dispute or lawsuit, we understand.

If you have placed your hope and trust for life on Jesus Christ, your hope might seem unreasonable, but that doesn't make it invalid. It has more validity than any other hope you can have because it is based on God's Word and promise. God cannot swear by anything or anyone greater than himself!

But it gets even better. Verse 17 says that God declared his oath out of a desire to make the unchanging nature of his purpose clear to the heirs of what was promised. In other words, God made the oath for our benefit! The heirs of the promise are those who put their faith in God through

Jesus Christ. He says the promise of God is for the benefit of these people. God didn't have to make any promises at all, but because he is gracious and full of mercy, he wanted to make it crystal clear to his people that his purposes never change, even though people and situations change all the time, for better or worse.

Every time you hear the promise of God in Scripture, take it as a reminder that his purposes and promises are rock solid and there is no power that can change them. Every promise of Scripture was confirmed by God when he sent Jesus to the cross. That's why Paul can say in 2 Corinthians 1:20 that all the promises of God are "yes" in Jesus Christ. Hope in God might seem unreasonable, but it is valid. Therefore, we should know the encouragement of hope.

ENCOURAGING HOPE

God confirmed his promise with an oath,

> so that by two unchangeable things, in which it is impossible for God to lie, we who have fled for refuge might have strong encouragement to hold fast to the hope set before us. We have this as a sure and steadfast anchor of the soul, a hope that enters into the inner place behind the curtain, where Jesus has gone as a forerunner on our behalf, having become a high priest forever after the order of Melchizedek. (6:18-20)

The two unchangeable things are God's promise and the oath that confirms it. Previously, the Pastor called the followers of Jesus "heirs of the promise." Now he uses another descriptive term, saying that we who follow Jesus are those who have "fled for refuge." Christians are those who have fled for safety in God, not out of fear, but because of God's promise. Christians are those who realize security is found only in the promise of God. There is no other promise more solid than his. What God wants is for his refugees to be encouraged and seize the hope he has set before them.

The Pastor uses an active term here. Hope has been set before you. Seize it. Grab it and don't let go. In other words, he is saying, "Keep hope alive!" Don't let go of your hope. He's just building on what he said in 6:11 when he stated that he longed for them to have an earnestness about the full assurance of hope all the way to the end. What the Pastor knows is that hope is a decision that must be made on a regular basis. If I have turned away from entrusting my life to myself and have turned to God in faith entrusting my life to Jesus Christ, I belong to him forever, and that will never change. However, my confidence and hope in God can waver dramatically. We have a daily need to hold on to our hope, and God wants us to have strong encouragement to do just that.

Why do we need this strong encouragement to seize the hope that God has set before us? Because hope is a sure and steadfast anchor of the soul. A ship that is anchored firmly and securely will not move from its location no matter what the waters are like. Whether the sea is calm, or the storm is raging, the firmly anchored ship holds steady. The hope God offers brings security to your soul, your life. Be encouraged to keep hope alive, to hold to God's unchanging hand, so that you will not be thrown into a frenzy when the storms of life are raging.

To take this point even further, we need this strong encouragement because the hope God offers is already and it is not yet. Christ having come into this world allows us to taste hope in part, but its fullness has yet to come. Jesus is the fulfillment of our hope, and he has already come and gone ahead of us as our forerunner that we might follow him into the inner place behind the curtain.

This strong encouragement to seize hope daily happens as we go where the hope takes us. This hope, the Pastor says, enters into the inner place behind the curtain. That is, by this hope we enter into the very throne of God. The curtain is a reference to the fabric in the temple that separated the most holy place in the temple from the people. Behind it dwelt the unadulterated presence of God. When the high priest entered that place, he only entered once per year, and he never came empty handed. He came with the blood of a sacrificial lamb.

The Pastor describes it this way in Hebrews 9:11-14:

> But when Christ appeared as a high priest of the good things that have come, then through the greater and more perfect tent (not made with hands, that is, not of this creation) he entered once for all into the holy places, not by means of the blood of goats and calves but by means of his own blood, thus securing an eternal redemption. For if the blood of goats and bulls, and the sprinkling of defiled persons with the ashes of a heifer, sanctify for the purification of the flesh, how much more will the blood of Christ, who through the eternal Spirit offered himself without blemish to God, purify our conscience from dead works to serve the living God.

Jesus made purification for sins and sat down at the right hand of the Majesty on high (Hebrews 1:3; 10:12). He's there right now, and we presently experience the benefits of that reality: Jesus, our great high priest, interceding, mediating with God the Father for us. That's reason enough for strong encouragement.

Do you understand the privilege you have as a Christian? We can become so bedazzled by the here and now that our eyes grow dim to the unequaled privilege that is following the Savior into God's presence. Jesus has opened up the way to live beyond the veil in the presence of God and he calls us to follow him there. That is why the Pastor said in 4:16, "Let us continually draw near, let us continually approach the throne of God with confidence that we may receive mercy and find grace to help in time of need" (author's translation). It's also how he can say in Hebrews 10:22, "Let us draw near with a true heart in full assurance of faith," and in 10:25, "Let us not neglect to meet together, as is the habit of some, but encouraging one another, all the more as you see the Day drawing near" (author's translation).

Hope takes us to prayer, worship, and fellowship with others who want to keep holding on to the hope. The assurance of hope has a practical, on-the-ground application that's implied by what the Pastor said in Hebrews 6:9-12:

> Though we speak in this way, yet in your case, beloved, we feel sure of better things—things that belong to salvation. For God is not unjust so as to overlook your work and the love that you have shown for his name in serving the saints, as you still do. And we desire each one of you to show the same earnestness to have the full assurance of hope until the end, so that you may not be sluggish, but imitators of those who through faith and patience inherit the promises.

What does the assurance of hope look like? A public faith that shows our love for God in the way we love our sisters and brothers in Christ. Our love for God as Christians is shown in the way that we love all people, but the Pastor is making a particular point about how Christian hope bears witness to the world that Jesus is real and worthy of worship. He reminds his readers that they have demonstrated time and again their love for God's name by the way they have earnestly served their brothers and sisters in Christ.

And they haven't stopped. They continue to do it. This love is a costly and self-sacrificial love, which he reminds them in 10:32-34:

> But recall the former days when, after you were enlightened, you endured a hard struggle with sufferings, sometimes being publicly exposed to reproach and affliction, and sometimes being partners with those so treated. For you had compassion on those in prison, and you joyfully accepted the plundering of your property, since you knew that you yourselves had a better possession and an abiding one.

Sacrificial Christian love demonstrates to the world that as unreasonable as Christian hope might appear to be, it is rooted in something far better than anything this world has to offer.

How might this kind of love for one another demonstrate the beauty of our unreasonable hope? Christian community is not a human creation. It is brought into being by the Spirit of God. He is the one who shines God's light into our hearts, bringing us out of darkness and into his kingdom (2 Corinthians 4:6; Colossians 1:13). Christians, then, share a familial bond with people whom they may have no connection with apart from faith in Jesus Christ. We naturally desire to build community with others based on all sorts of preferences and affinities. But that's not how God operates! While the divisiveness of our current culture around race, politics, gender identity, and sexuality drive people to associate primarily (or solely!) with those who share their convictions, Christian hope presses in the opposite direction. Rooted in God's love, it overflows in love for one another expressed in desiring and pursuing unity in our diversity. Again, we are to be eager to maintain the unity of the Spirit in the bond of peace because Christians are called to one hope (Ephesians 4:3-4).

Are you a Christian? Are you able to sacrificially love other Christians who think differently than you on social and political issues? Or do you lean into the cultural trend of only associating with Christians who share your perspectives? The one hope that binds us is unreasonable and glorious at the same time in the way that it shows forth the reconciling, persevering power of Jesus Christ.

5

THE PERFECT HOPE

The people knew that God could condemn the best of them.
They also knew that the priest could redeem the worst of them.

REV. RUSSELL WHITFIELD,
"THE DAY OF ATONEMENT"

I was a young man in the early 1990s when Toyota launched Lexus, their luxury vehicle brand. I was captivated by their advertising slogan. Every print ad and commercial boldly declared their commitment: "The Relentless Pursuit of Perfection." The advertising company Toyota hired to prepare for the launch of Lexus didn't just pluck that slogan out of thin air. When they visited Lexus designers in Japan, they noticed the designer's obsessive attention to detail. They pursued perfection in every aspect of this vehicle. Of course, their slogan had to be the relentless *pursuit* of perfection because they knew that perfection couldn't actually be attained, but they'd never stop pursuing it. And guess what? We're two decades into the twenty-first century and Lexus is no closer to perfection than they were in 1990.

That shouldn't surprise any of us. We know perfection is neither practical nor possible. These days people like to post workout clips on Instagram and TikTok overlayed with motivational speaker Les Brown saying, "Practice, and practice, and practice." Then he asks the audience, "Practice makes what?" The audience replies, "Perfect." Brown declares,

"Absolutely not! Dismantle that belief system." Then comes the money line: "Practice makes improvement. You can always better your best." Brown makes it clear that we will be *pursuing* perfection, never arriving at it.

Maybe Christians should take that approach when setting our expectations. Maybe Christians should be content with the *pursuit* of perfection in matters of justice, shalom, unity, and fellowship. In some sense, this is the most reasonable approach. Christians, like Israel prior to entering the Promised Land, exist in liminal space. We're citizens of a kingdom that has not yet arrived in full measure. We long for justice as we await the coming day of peace. Perfection is still on the way.

But when we look at the Pastor's emphasis in the middle chapter of Hebrews, he seems obsessed by the concept of perfection. He's not focusing on perfection because he believes it is impossible to attain. Rather, he's focused on it because he wants the Hebrews to be absolutely clear that perfection is required but only attainable through the ministry of the perfect high priest, Jesus Christ. He's beginning to dig into the importance of Jesus' ministry as a high priest, and the first stop on his tour is the message about perfection.

Jesus' ministry as a high priest is not a new subject introduced in chapter 7. In chapter 2, the Pastor began to declare that the ascended, glorified Jesus was a merciful and faithful high priest in the service of God. In fact, chapters 1, 11, and 12 are the only ones where the Pastor does not explicitly refer to Jesus as a high priest or a great priest. Jesus' priestly ministry is essential to Christian hope! Jesus holds his priesthood permanently and always lives to make intersession for his people (Hebrews 7:24-25).

The nuance the Pastor details in chapters 5–7 is that Jesus is a high priest after the order of Melchizedek (Hebrews 5:6, 10; 6:20; 7:11, 15, 17). At the end of chapter 6, our hope is explicitly tied to Jesus' priesthood. Hope is a sure and steadfast anchor of the soul because it enters into the most holy place of the heavenly temple. That's where Jesus has gone ahead of us on our behalf, a high priest after the order of Melchizedek (Hebrews 6:19-20). However, it's not that Jesus' priesthood is a copy of Melchizedek's. Jesus is the original and Melchizedek is the copy! The Pastor takes great pains to demonstrate the excellence of Melchizedek so that his people will joyfully invest their lives in Jesus. Melchizedek, as priest of God Most High, is the copy of the unique high priest, Jesus Christ. He gives his readers indisputable evidence of how great the copy is to remove any doubt that the original is even better.

From chapter 1 all the way through the letter, the Pastor has quoted directly from or referred to the Old Testament repeatedly.[1] And now, in the first three verses of chapter 7, he takes us back again by summarizing Genesis 14. In keeping with his previous goal, he continues to focus attention on the reality that the Old Testament is Christ-centered. That is, to read the Old Testament and miss Jesus is to miss the whole point. Why else would he spend time talking about Melchizedek who is only mentioned two times in the Old Testament? For the same reason that he talked about Moses, Abraham, and the Psalms—so that he can talk about Jesus!

His readers are facing temptation to be drawn back under the rules and regulations of the old covenant. That temptation includes going back under the Levitical priesthood. And he wants them to know that would be a tragic mistake because the old covenant—the "Old Testament"—was itself all about Jesus. So even when the Bible mentions the encounter between Abraham and this mysterious man Melchizedek, the Holy Spirit's intention is to teach us something about Jesus. Even there, the Holy Spirit's aim is to testify to the greatness of the Son of God. You see, the Pastor is not doing theological gymnastics by pointing to Jesus through Genesis 14. He's not trying to show them how theologically sharp he is. What he wants to do is encourage their faith in Jesus. "Don't you dare think about turning away from following Jesus. You have not believed a lie!" Every time you and I open our Bible, we should see Jesus.

THE KING OF RIGHTEOUSNESS AND PEACE

The Pastor wanted to start talking about Jesus as a high priest after the order of Melchizedek back in chapter 5, but he had a few things to say before he could get back to the topic. He's concluded the digression he took from 5:11–6:20, and now, he jumps back in with both feet when says in verses 1-3,

> For this Melchizedek, king of Salem, priest of the Most High God, met Abraham returning from the slaughter of the kings and blessed him, and to him Abraham apportioned a tenth part of everything. He is first, by translation of his name, king of righteousness, and then he is also king of Salem, that is, king of peace. He is without father or mother or genealogy, having neither beginning of days nor end of life, but resembling the Son of God he continues a priest forever.

When the battle of the kings took place in Genesis 14 and Sodom fell, Lot, Abraham's nephew, was taken captive along with all his possessions. Abraham then took his own army of 318 men and defeated the cohort of kings who had taken his nephew. When he returned from the slaughter of kings, the king of Sodom came out to meet him. But so did this other king, Melchizedek, the king of Salem. Melchizedek had prepared a celebratory meal. It says that he brought out bread and wine. But the Pastor doesn't mention the bread and wine here. He's more interested in doing a little Hebrew translation for us.

He points out first how to translate Melchizedek's name. He says, he is first, by translation of his name, king of righteousness. The Hebrew word for "king" is *mẹlẹk*, and the Hebrew word for "righteousness" is *tsẹdẹq*. If you were to open your Hebrew Bible and read Genesis 14:18, you would read *malki-tsẹdẹq*. So first, he says, I want you to understand that after his victory, Abraham met up with a man whose name means "king of righteousness." The king of Sodom was there too, but Abraham dismissed him. The man he paid homage to was the king of righteousness. But not only that, the king of righteousness was also the king of peace. He was also *mẹlẹḵ shalem*. *Shalem* has the same Hebrew letters that make up the word *shalom* but with different vowels. In the original manuscript of Genesis 14, there wouldn't have been any vowels at all. All you would've seen are the three letters. So the Pastor says that the king of Salem was also the king of peace.

Abraham, the father of the faithful, tithed a tenth of all the spoils he got from the victory to this man who was "king of righteousness and peace." And here's the kicker—in verse 3, the Pastor says that this king of righteousness and peace is "without father or mother or genealogy." He has neither beginning of days nor end of life. His point is not that Melchizedek literally didn't have a father or mother, or that he didn't die. He's making an argument from silence. The Bible says nothing about Melchizedek's genealogy. And that's a striking point. Why? Because Genesis is full of genealogies. In fact, the book is divided into ten chapters of genealogies (Genesis 2:4; 5:1; 6:9; 10:1; 11:10, 27; 25:12, 19; 36:1; 37:2). In a book concerned with generations and genealogies, for this king of righteousness and peace to be missing a genealogical record is striking. He is presented to us as someone who is *timeless*. In this way, the Pastor says, he resembles the Son of God.

Melchizedek is the copy and Jesus is the reality. Melchizedek is mentioned in Scripture long before Jesus, but Jesus is still the original and Melchizedek is still the copy. So, if Abraham paid homage to this man who was the king of righteousness and peace, and this man was only a copy of the real deal, how much more are we to recognize and bow down to the true king of righteousness and peace, Jesus Christ?

Jesus is the Prince of Peace who establishes his kingdom and upholds it with justice and righteousness (Isaiah 9:6-7). The Pastor is reinforcing what he has already said about Jesus when he quoted from Psalm 45 in 1:8-9:

> But of the Son he says, "Your throne, O God, is forever and ever, the scepter of uprightness is the scepter of your kingdom. You

have loved righteousness and hated wickedness; therefore God, your God, has anointed you with the oil of gladness beyond your companions."

Jesus is better because he is the true king whose kingdom is marked by righteousness and peace, and that will go right over our heads unless we understand our need for a unique high priest who will not die.

OUR UNIQUE HIGH PRIEST

The Pastor points to Melchizedek not only because he was a king, but particularly because he was a priest of the Most High God. The fact that there is no record of his birth or death in Scripture makes his priesthood uniquely resemble the priesthood of the Son of God because it continues forever. Hebrews 7:4 emphasizes this point when the Pastor effectively writes, "Do you get how great this man was!" The structure of the verse in Greek emphasizes Melchizedek's superiority to Abraham. If we were to translate according to its word order, it would read, "So you see how great this man was to whom Abraham gave a tenth of the spoils, the patriarch!" If Abraham willingly acknowledged that this man was an authentic priest of God, that settles the matter. There was no law at the time requiring Abraham to give a tithe to this man, and he didn't give Melchizedek the scraps of what was left over. The word translated as "spoils" describes the top of the heap. He gave Melchizedek from the best of what he had, and he did it freely and willingly, without compulsion, recognizing that this man was God's priest.

Beginning in 7:5, the Pastor pauses to explain the point that he's making. The priests in Israel came from the tribe of Levi, one of Jacob's twelve sons. That makes Abraham Levi's great-grandfather. The Pastor intentionally takes it back to Levi to get as close to Abraham as possible. The priests of Israel were Levites, yes, but they were specifically descended from Aaron, who was the first high priest. But the Levites were the only one of the twelve tribes that did not receive any inheritance of land. They were set apart by God to remain responsible for the holy things in Israel. So, everything in the tabernacle was cared for by Levites. Not only that, but they were responsible for collecting the tithe from their fellow Israelites for their livelihood, of which they gave a tithe to the descendants of Aaron, who were the priests.

At this point, the Pastor's readers would've been nodding their heads in agreement, which is why what he says in the next two verses is so important.

> But this man who does not have his descent from them received tithes from Abraham and blessed him who had the promises. It is beyond dispute that the inferior is blessed by the superior. In the one case tithes are received by mortal men, but in the other case, by one of whom it is testified that he lives. (7:6-8)

When you have a priest who lives forever, how can you even think of going back to a system of giving tithes to men who will die? Jesus is a unique and superior high priest in Jesus, and the Pastor is urging them against returning to what God has replaced with Christ! Why is it significant for us to know Christ's unique and better work as high priest?

For a modern audience, this line of argument may lose some of its punch, as the Pastor's readers knew that they needed a priest. We might criticize their ancient culture, but they were clear on the necessity of righteousness, holiness, and godliness. Those weren't terms they could easily dismiss the way we do so often today. For them, the Levitical priesthood was everything. As Pastor Russ Whitfield put it, "The people knew that God could condemn the best of them. They also knew that the priest could redeem the worst of them."[2] That's why they were so drawn to return to the priestly system. We are disconnected from that pull and far more likely to take a cavalier attitude toward righteousness and holiness, but they were not. They knew their state and understood it required a priest to mediate between them and God. What they needed, however, was to have their attention refocused on the right priest.

Back in 2:14-18, the Pastor first highlighted need, saying,

> Since therefore the children share in flesh and blood, he himself likewise partook of the same things, that through death he might destroy the one who has the power of death, that is, the devil, and deliver all those who through fear of death were subject to lifelong slavery. For surely it is not angels that he helps, but he helps the offspring of Abraham. Therefore he had to be made like his brothers in every respect, so that he might become a merciful and faithful high priest in the service of God, to make propitiation for the sins of the people. For because he himself has suffered when tempted, he is able to help those who are being tempted.

Jesus, through his death and resurrection, has been established as a priest forever to continually deliver us from our enslavement to sin.

Where Melchizedek met Abraham in the flesh, they meet again in Jesus Christ. As P. E. Hughes says,

> Thus, as both Son of man and Son of God, Christ bridges the gulf which separates man and his guilt on the one side and God and his righteousness on the other; by his atoning priestly sacrifice of himself on the cross he fulfils the requirements for a reconciliation that is complete and everlasting; and in his exaltation the glory of the Son of God becomes also the glory of the Son of man and of all those sons of men who through faith are forever made one with him.[3]

See how great Jesus is? It was both necessary and fitting for him to become a uniquely great high priest. God wants us to understand that, embrace it, and rejoice in it.

THE IMPERFECT CONDITION

Michael Kenneth Williams became a famous actor in the early 2000s playing Omar in the HBO series *The Wire*. He died of a drug overdose on September 6, 2021, in Brooklyn at the age of fifty-four. He struggled with drug addiction for most of his adult life and did not know that the heroin he purchased had been laced with a lethal amount of fentanyl.[4] Williams's addiction was rooted in childhood trauma. He was molested as an adolescent and thought of himself as damaged goods.

In a 2016 interview with National Public Radio's Terry Gross, Williams described his relationship with Reverend Ronald Christian and his experience at Christian Love Baptist Church in New Jersey. He met Rev. Christian during the second season of *The Wire* when he was on a downward spiral of abusing drugs. He was, in his own words, in jeopardy of destroying everything he had worked for.

> I'm not saying that he accepted me in my dysfunctionalism, but he loved me in it. . . . That was the first time I actually walked in a church and felt okay. I didn't feel dirty. I would never go into a church. It made me question myself on every level. Those events happening so early on in my life. And I would go to church with this secret, this weight. Like, I'm dirty. I'm dirty. God is never going to want me. I'm dirty. I had a very low self-esteem coming up and I just never felt like God loves me because I was dirty. I was damaged goods. . . . And I wore that badge very early on in my life. And I didn't let that go until I walked into Christian Love Baptist Church. I saw other men who said, "Me too," out loud. And it doesn't make you less of a man. It doesn't make you dirty. Learning how to forgive myself and forgive other people. I got all of that at Christian Love.[5]

There's a lot we could say about what Williams shared, but here's why I'm bringing up this story. Whether or not you are able to relate to his experience, no one gets through this life trauma free.

No matter how wealthy or successful you are by society's standards, no matter how displaced you may be from the pathway to prosperity, none of us gets to live a life without the need for continual healing—physical, emotional, mental, and spiritual healing. Pain and trauma are pervasive in the human experience. We suffer pain, and we cause pain. We are traumatized, and we traumatize others. Where do we find hope for this seemingly permanent problem? We are clear on our imperfection, but we are unclear about the demand for perfection. We are even less clear about our need for a priest as the solution to our imperfect condition.

The Pastor directs our eyes to the greatness of Jesus Christ by pointing out the imperfect condition that existed under the Levitical priesthood. The original readers of this letter centered their entire life of worship around the priesthood. When they became Christians, it was a radical change from what they knew in terms of life and worship. We can relate to the temptation to drift back toward what is comfortable.

That's why the Pastor doubles down with an incredible statement:

> Now if perfection had been attainable through the Levitical priesthood (for under it the people received the law), what further need would there have been for another priest to arise after the order of Melchizedek, rather than one named after the order of Aaron? (Hebrews 7:11)

The people received the law from God through the Levitical priesthood, which was established by God, but it was never God's plan that perfection would be secured through it. Don't miss the importance of this statement. God's goal for us is perfection. That's his standard. So we need another priesthood because perfection could not be attained through the Levitical priesthood. You and I are *not* perfect, but that doesn't change God's standard.

At this point in the letter, the Pastor has only applied the concept of perfection to Christ (2:10; 5:9), but at the end of chapter 7, he says, "For the law appoints men in their weakness as high priests, but the word of the oath, which came later than the law, appoints a Son who has been made perfect forever" (7:28). The perfection at stake here is not about Jesus—it's about you and me. The problem is we don't fix our eyes high enough. We're quick to utter "I'm not perfect" whenever we need an excuse for our mistakes, but that doesn't change God's requirement of perfection. We are quick to content ourselves with imperfection and willing to excuse it away, but God is not. Oh, how this meets us in our weariness! Like the Lexus engineers, we toil and labor in the never-ending pursuit of perfection, but hope cannot be found in that kind of work. Our hope is in the one who is a high priest by the power of an indestructible life.

It must be so because the pursuit of perfection is regularly offensive to us. If you can read the Bible and not be offended by it, you're not being honest. Any time I read through the Law, particularly Leviticus and Numbers, I find myself offended by some of the regulations and the penalties God imposes for breaking the Law. Some of what I read rocks me to the core. But here's the thing: I'm offended, not because there's a problem with God or his Law, but because I don't fully grasp the implications of what it means to be holy. Like everyone else, I drift toward equating niceness with godliness, but the Bible equates holiness with godliness.

Jesus did not die on the cross to make a bunch of nice people. He died on the cross because there was no other way for people to be made perfect in holiness. It wouldn't have been necessary for another priest to come along after the order of Melchizedek if perfection was possible through the one named after the order of Aaron. But that one was temporary.

THE PERFECT HOPE

There's been a change in priesthood because of the need for perfection. In 7:12, the Pastor notes that when there's a change in the priesthood, there is necessarily a change in the law as well. In other words, Jesus is a different kind of priest. That old priesthood is null and void. "For the one of whom these things are spoken belonged to another tribe, from which no one has ever served at the altar. For it is evident that our Lord was descended from Judah, and in connection with that tribe Moses said nothing about priests" (vv. 13-14). His readers would've been asking, How can Jesus be priest?

He does not meet the requirement. He was not from the tribe of Levi; he was from the tribe of Judah.

But the Pastor anticipates their problem. The fact that God requires perfection makes it necessary for a priest to arise who was not associated with the tribe of Levi. God has resolved the imperfect condition with the perfect hope.

> This becomes even more evident when another priest arises in the likeness of Melchizedek, who has become a priest, not on the basis of a legal requirement concerning bodily descent, but by the power of an indestructible life. For it is witnessed of him, "You are a priest forever, after the order of Melchizedek." For on the one hand, a former commandment is set aside because of its weakness and use-lessness (for the law made nothing perfect); but on the other hand, a better hope is introduced, through which we draw near to God. (Hebrews 7:15-19)

It was necessary for another priest to arise like Melchizedek because those who became priests through bodily descent could never be the solution to the problem. We needed a better hope. If perfection could've been attained through them, why were there so many of them? Priests always had a successor because they all eventually died (Hebrews 7:23)! Can you see how much better it is to have a priest who holds his priesthood per-manently by virtue of conquering death? He continues forever because he has become a priest by the power of an indestructible life!

Jesus is a better hope. Jesus is the best hope. Jesus is the perfect hope—because he's not dead! The cross was not the end. He lives now contin-ually, permanently, forever at the right hand of the Majesty on high. And he's not sitting there twiddling his thumbs, trying to find something to do. He is mediating, that is, interceding and ministering continually as the great high priest for all his people. The apostle Paul says in 1 Timothy 2:5, "There is one God, and there is one mediator between God and men, the man Christ Jesus." Do you see why Jesus' high priesthood is the perfect hope? Jesus, who is both God and man in one person, lives right now, and if you belong to him, he is ministering before the Father on your behalf.

That's why the Pastor could say so confidently in 2:18 that since Jesus suffered when tempted, he is able to help those who are being tempted. It's also why he says in 4:15,

> We do not have a high priest who is unable to sympathize with our weaknesses, but one who has in every respect been tempted as we have yet without sin. Let us then with confidence draw near to the throne of grace that we may receive mercy and find grace to help in time of need.

The goal is perfection because the goal is to draw near to God. He said as much in 4:14-16 and he makes the point twice here in chapter 7. According to verse 19, because Jesus is a priest forever after the order of Melchizedek, "a better hope is introduced, through which we draw near to God." Then in verse 25, the Pastor explains that Jesus' permanent priesthood means "he is able to save to the uttermost those who draw near to God through him, since he always lives to make intercession for them." That's why the goal of life isn't niceness. No—the goal of life is to worship in the presence of God. If we are conscious of this better hope, if we possess this better hope, we find joy, peace, and comfort in the reality that our lives are lived before the face of God.

Entering into the inner place, behind the curtain, into the very presence of God, is the Christian's daily reality (Hebrews 6:19-20). Jesus' ministry of perfecting his people involves qualifying them to draw near to God. This is the better hope. This is the perfect hope. You and I must grasp this hope. God desires for his people to seize it as he has set it before us (6:18). You've got to because the Pastor is not going to get off this train of connecting perfection in Christ with the goal of drawing near to God.

1. "How much more will the blood of Christ, who through the eternal Spirit offered himself without blemish to God, purify

our conscience from dead works to serve the living God" (Hebrews 9:14).

2. "For since the law has but a shadow of the good things to come instead of the true form of these realities, it can never, by the same sacrifices that are continually offered every year, make perfect those who draw near" (Hebrews 10:1).

3. "And since we have a great priest over the house of God, let us draw near with a true heart in full assurance of faith, with our hearts sprinkled clean from an evil conscience and our bodies washed with pure water" (Hebrews 10:20-22).

The Pastor can talk so confidently about drawing near to God because the basis of that hope is the unshakable oath between God the Father and God the Son.

The Son, Jesus Christ, is the one who has been made perfect forever. And just like the Pastor does at the beginning of the letter when he places the words of Psalm 110:1 in the mouth of the Father spoken to the Son, he does so again here in chapter 7 by quoting Psalm 110:4: "The Lord has sworn and will not change his mind, 'You are a priest forever.'" This makes Jesus the guarantor of a better covenant" (Hebrews 7:21-22). We'll explore that in more detail in the next chapter, but after stating the unshakable ground of the oath between the Father and the Son, the Pastor turns his attention to the Son's perfection.

THE PERFECT ONE

It almost seems anticlimactic to talk about Jesus as the perfect one. We've already established that the way to the perfection God requires is through Jesus Christ, who is a priest of another order who can accomplish what the Levitical priesthood could not accomplish. Why not take Jesus' perfection as the necessary conclusion to what he's already said? Why tell them "the word of the oath, which came later than the law, appoints a Son who has been made perfect forever" (7:28)? Not only that, but how could Jesus be made perfect? If he's God, then he's already perfect. In his humanity, 7:26 describes him as holy, innocent, unstained, and separated from sinners. If that doesn't describe perfect, I don't know what does!

Here's the deal: if you are going to endure, you need to know why Jesus' ministry is so effective. Why is he a fitting high priest, and why is his work so effective? The Pastor repeats himself again here at the end of chapter 7. This repetition is God's grace to us. For the third time in the letter, he reinforces Jesus' street cred.

If you're going to follow somebody, it's best to know they've got some credibility. It's best to know that they earned their spot. If you're going to get financial and investment advice, it's better to go to somebody like Warren Buffet than it is to talk to the winner of the latest Mega Millions lottery. Both have a lot of money, but only one has credibility. Only one has learned how to work the system to their advantage.

This is the third time the Pastor has said that Jesus was *made* perfect (2:10; 5:8-9; 7:27-28). He is reinforcing our sense of confidence that we're following the right one. Jesus is qualified to lead his people to the throne of God because he was perfected in the school of hard knocks. His credentials came through his suffering. He's not a high priest who is separated from our suffering. He's separated from our sin, but he knows our suffering intimately.

Every time the Pastor talks about Jesus' perfection, he connects it with Jesus' suffering. In 2:10, he was made perfect through suffering. In 5:8, he learned obedience through what he suffered. And here in 7:27, he has no need to offer up daily sacrifices for his own sins before those of the people since he offered up himself as the one-time, all-sufficient sacrifice for the people.

He's the perfect one, but not in a way that is disconnected from us. He's the perfect one for us to follow on our way to perfection. The priests of old stood every day offering the same sacrifices (Hebrews 10:11). The great high priest, Jesus Christ, took his seat on the throne after making one sacrifice for all time so that his people would be perfect and sanctified for all time (Hebrews 10:12). And look at what we hear in Hebrews 10:14, "For by a single offering he has perfected for all time those who are being sanctified."

We're quick to say we're not perfect as a way of excusing our imperfections. There's a Christian cliché that goes something like this, "I'm not perfect, just forgiven." But the Pastor says something radical here! When we think about perfection, we think about heaven. We think about the promise of the new heavens and earth where the impact of sin on the world is completely gone. That's when perfection comes, right? In one sense, yes. But Hebrews 10:14 is a shock-and-awe truth about what it means to be a Christian. By a single offering, Jesus Christ *has perfected* for all time those who are being sanctified.

Are you a Christian? You're not just forgiven, you're perfect. If it wasn't right here, plain as day, you wouldn't believe me. If it wasn't right here, plain as day, you *shouldn't* believe me. Even though it's written in the Bible, you still might have a hard time believing me. To say that a Christian is perfect sounds like the height of arrogance, as it seems to imply that Christians are "first class" and non-Christians are "second class." And besides, I know my thoughts. I know what goes on in my mind and in my heart. I know what goes on in the lives of other people who say they're Christians, and *perfect* is not the word I would use to describe either myself or them. But none of that changes the fact that perfection for the Christian is described here as an accomplished goal.

This is God's perspective about you if you are in Christ. That is, if you are united to Jesus Christ by faith, from God's point of view you have been made perfect. It isn't a goal that you accomplished. It's a goal that Jesus accomplished for you. The Pastor wants his readers to know that Jesus, who was made perfect through suffering, by his single sacrifice, has done what the law could not do. He has brought perfection to his people. Far from being a statement of arrogance or pride, it is humbling to consider the fact that in all our mess anyone could say that we were perfect. But God says it about the Christian.

Even as the Pastor speaks of perfection as an already accomplished goal, he describes the process that's taking place. Who has Jesus perfected? Those who are being sanctified, meaning those who are being made holy. How is it that the Christian can be declared perfect? How does this sanctification happen? Jesus Christ created a relationship focused on what we remember and what God forgets. By faith, he places his laws on our hearts and in our minds. God's Word starts working on our insides. We remember it. It comes to mind as we live. It begins to shape and form our attitude and actions. We can't get away from it. While we remember his Word, he forgets our sins and lawless deeds. Not for a little while. Not for a year or a day, but forever. Is there a better deal than that anywhere?

When Jesus washed his disciples' feet in John 13:6-10, Peter objected and said, "You shall never wash my feet." Jesus said to him, "If I do not wash you, you have no share with me." Then Peter said, "Don't just wash my feet, but do my hands and my head too!" And Jesus, because he knew that his once-for-all sacrifice would carry away their sins forever, said to his disciples, "You are clean." Christian, Jesus has taken his seat. There is no more offering for sin. There is only forgiveness. You are clean.

Everyone who follows Jesus is declared perfect and is engaged in the relentless pursuit of perfection. God's work of conforming us to the image of his Son motivates us to lay aside every weight and sin which so easily besets us and run with endurance the race set before us, looking to Jesus, the founder and perfecter of our faith (Hebrews 12:1-3). The Pastor won't allow us to ignore God's goal of perfection because he knows that the cost of growing in holiness is high. Salvation is free, but it's not cheap. It costs us everything. But seeing the perfect Savior who brings us to life before the face of God makes us willing to give all of ourselves to him.

6

THE BETTER HOPE

And while there is much to critique and criticize in our lonely civilization, this is a movement built on inextinguishable hope.

ANDY CROUCH, *THE LIFE WE'RE LOOKING FOR*

I've been a sports fan as long as I can remember and have enjoyed many a good sports movie. My earliest sports film recollection is one by Warren Beatty called *Heaven Can Wait*. Beatty's character was named Joe Pendleton. He was the star quarterback for the Los Angeles Rams and on the verge of leading his team to the Super Bowl when he is struck by a truck while riding his bike. An overzealous angel prematurely removes him from his body, assuming that he was about to die. When he arrives in heaven, Joe refuses to believe that his time is up. So, he pleads his case that he needs more time on earth. He successfully argues his point with the overzealous angel's supervisor, but there's a problem—he can't go back into his original body because it's been cremated. So, they have to find another dead body for him to enter. Lo and behold, there's this multi-millionaire who's just died, murdered by an unfaithful wife.

Joe comes back to life in the multi-millionaire's body. Then he buys the Rams so that he can become their starting quarterback and lead them to the Super Bowl. The problem is that his wife still wants him dead. Right before the Super Bowl, he's shot. The Rams are forced to start the backup quarterback, but during the game the backup takes a brutal hit, and guess what happens? He dies. What happens after that? Right again. The angel's supervisor sends Joe into the backup quarterback's body, and he leads the Rams to Super Bowl victory.

At this point, you're probably wondering what this story has to do with hope? I'm glad you asked. The message of the movie is that heaven can wait because it can't possibly be better than getting what we want right now. Attaining a lifelong dream—that's heaven! But the truth is when I do get what I want, I find out that there's something else I want that's even better.

In Hebrews, the Pastor demonstrates that there's nothing better in the present life than the heavenly reality granted to those who have Jesus as their great high priest. As he presses even further in on the glory of Jesus' priestly ministry, his message is that life is better in Christ now. It's not simply that everything's going to be better in heaven, so you've got to keep grinding through the life on earth until you get there. There's some truth to that, but his message is that the reality of heaven has broken into the present and that makes all the difference in the world for God's people. So he fixes the gaze and focus of his readers on heavenly realities so that they will understand its impact on them right now.

IT'S ALL BETTER

What makes life better? There are as many answers to that question as there are people. However, when I say "better," I don't mean "easier." When it comes to new technology, advertisers promise that the latest product will make our lives better through ease, convenience, comfort, and material prosperity. It'll give me more control over my life. New technology has completely changed our day to day, making many things easier in a more connected world. But is life necessarily better because things are new or easier? The stress that comes with constant connection via technology is well testified. We're not made to be "on" all the time. So you can't just assume that new technology means a better life. Still, it is easy for our view of a better life to be tethered to our perception of how much control we have. The thought is that life becomes better to the degree that I can exercise control over everything from my self-definition to my environment.

During my undergraduate years I memorized the poem "Invictus," written by William Ernest Henley in 1875. The last stanza of the poem declares,

> It matters not how straight the gate,
> How charged with punishment the scroll,
> I am the master of my fate,
> I am the captain of my soul.

It is a fist-shaking defiance in the face of adversity. "I thank whatever gods may be for my unconquerable soul," he writes in the first stanza. Every human heart resonates with the desire to be the master and captain of our lives. We find ourselves making declarations like this in response to the wearying battle for control. There are certainly times when the ability to summon this kind of defiant resilience in the face of adversity is a benefit.

On January 1, 2023, actor Jeremy Renner was tragically crushed under the steel tracks of his fourteen-thousand-pound snowcat. His body was literally broken from toe to head, and he groaned in agony for every breath. His neighbors and nephew desperately tended to him, exhorting him to hold on as they waited for emergency medical services to make their way through the snow and render aid. Miraculously, he survived. Diane Sawyer interviewed Jeremy and his family just a few months after the accident. She asked the family, "Are you amazed by this recovery? What do you attribute it to?" Jeremy's sister, Kim, said, "Yeah. It's just being stubborn as [bleep]." "That's 100 percent what it is," another family member chimed in. "He's not going to let anything take him down." Jeremy laughed and said, "I have that tenacious belief." Sawyer replied, "I mean, this is like Hawkeye belief."[1] "Well, I don't know. It's just belief, man," was Renner's response. "His fellow superheroes and friends already know that about him," Sawyer tells us. "Jeremy Renner does not give up."[2]

Whether or not Renner is familiar with "Invictus," that's the kind of fight he displayed while on the precipice of death. And it likely played a role in saving his life. At the same time, if his neighbors weren't in their garage with the door partly open to allow his nephew to slide under and beg for help, if the wind hadn't died down just enough to allow the medical helicopter to land and transport him to the hospital, no level of personal resilience would have saved his life. Renner, of course, is aware of this miraculous confluence of events. Friends, defiant resilience in the face of adversity may be a benefit but is unable to control life and make it better.

Dr. Elissa Epel is a world-renowned psychologist and expert on stress. In her book *The Stress Prescription,* she writes, "A sense of control is one of the pivotal factors that drives our stress levels up and down. We *love control.* . . . We want to know our future. And not only to *know* it, but to have the power to determine how it unfolds to the greatest extent possible."[3] Even though feeling a sense of control helps to regulate our emotions, Dr. Epel points out that it is a double-edged sword. We respond to the uncertainty of life by attempting to exert more control so that our lives become more predictable and safer, which makes stress more of a constant in our lives and toxic to us.[4]

When it comes to God's promise of a better life, better is not determined by the measure of control we are able to exercise over it. That's the problem with the readers of Hebrews. I can hear them talking to the Pastor now. "You sold us a bill of goods! This whole life with Jesus is supposed to be better, but we're catching hell!" They, like us, have to readjust their definition of better.

The Pastor wants to encourage his readers about the blessings they have as followers of Jesus Christ. Jesus is the great high priest who has passed through the heavens, who stands between us and the Father having paid the price for our sins, who eases our fear of God, and who strengthens us to endure. Life with Christ is better because he's better. When you're in the middle of a struggle, things always seem worse because you are not in control of the outcome. In a boxing match, the rounds are just three minutes, but if you're getting beat up, that three minutes can seem like a lifetime. All you want is to hear the bell ring!

The Pastor has the audacity to tell these folks in the middle of their fight why things are better. Things are better now because Jesus has a better ministry. He's the mediator of a better covenant that is built on better promises. This is true even though their struggles remain.

BETTER MINISTRY

People think a lot of things about Jesus, but rarely do you hear anyone refer to him as a minister. Yet, that's exactly how the Pastor describes him beginning in chapter 8.

> Now the point in what we are saying is this: we have such a high priest, one who is seated at the right hand of the throne of the Majesty in heaven, a minister in the holy places, in the true tent that the Lord set up, not man. (8:1-2)

He has just shown in chapter 7 that Jesus is the perfect high priest—a priest forever after the order of Melchizedek. Then, in the very next breath he summarizes his point to make it as clear as possible. This perfect high priest is ours.

What's significant about Jesus sitting down is that the priests who served in the tabernacle were continually making offerings for the people: burnt offerings, guilt offerings, peace offerings, sin offerings, bulls, goats, lambs, rams, even grain. Every day blood was shed in the tabernacle so that the people would not be consumed by their holy God. Thus, the Pastor rightly says, "Every high priest is appointed to offer gifts and sacrifices" (8:3). Notice the difference when he talks about Jesus. In comparison he says, "Thus it is necessary for this priest also to have some*thing* to offer." Their offering is plural and ongoing. Jesus' offering is a singular, once-for-all offering for sin.

When he made his offering, it was finished. There was no longer any further offering for sin. Jesus took his seat, but that doesn't mean he's not working. His seat is not just the seat of rest from his work of sacrificing himself on our behalf. It is also the seat of ministry. And it's the best seat in the house. It is the seat of power and authority. It is his throne at the right hand of the Majesty in heaven.

The Pastor says Jesus is a minister in the holy places, in the true tabernacle that the Lord set up. He fixes the eyes of his readers heavenward. He's letting them know that they're missing the boat trying to return to the earthly temple as the focal point of their worship. That's just a copy and a shadow of the heavenly tabernacle. Here's what gets us every time— what we believe is what we can see with our eyes and touch with our hands. They could see this glorious temple in Jerusalem, and their hearts were drawn to it. The Pastor wants to shake them up and say that's not the original.

Jesus has a better ministry because he ministers with more authority in the true tabernacle. The Lord himself set this one up, not Moses. God the Son is right now, as you read this, ministering in the most holy place in the presence of God the Father on behalf of everyone who follows him. The Pastor is not talking theory or speculation. He is speaking fact. *We* have such a high priest.

The Pastor doesn't say, "You're blessed because I'm your pastor. You're blessed because I'm the man of God in this house." The ultimate blessing for any congregation is not the person who occupies the pulpit. The blessing is that Jesus is your senior pastor. Yes, Jesus appoints pastors and elders in his church. Yes, at the end of this letter, the Pastor will tell them in 13:17, "Obey your leaders and submit to them, for they are keeping watch over your souls, as those who will give an account." But he wants them to become preoccupied with the reality of Jesus' heavenly priestly and pastoral ministry.

The problem is that they are preoccupied with the transitory. They are focused on what Jesus describes as "treasures on earth, where moth and rust destroy and where thieves break in and steal." And this preoccupation with stuff that is not permanent, with something that is at best a copy and shadow of reality, hinders their faith. The glory and splendor of an earthly tabernacle cannot come close to matching the glory of the heavenly tabernacle. Jesus is ministering in the most beautiful place you can imagine. And his ministry there is more excellent because it produces the fruit of endurance.

Why is it, if you're a Christian, that you have not thrown in the towel in the middle of the fight? It's not because you are in control of the situation. It's because your ability to endure is the fruit of Jesus' more excellent ministry in the true tabernacle. Here is a practical way that this plays out negatively when we do not believe that endurance is the fruit of Jesus' better ministry. Social media platforms get blamed for everything from worsening political divides and providing a means of spying on citizens to enabling foreign governments to disrupt elections, destroying personal relationships, and devolving our cultural values. I'm sure there are other ways we can describe the undesirable influences social media has on our lives, but I would wager most users do not participate for any of those purposes. Our conscious reasons are things like connecting with other people, promoting ourselves or products, or becoming an influencer. Few of us will say that exercising control is a primary motive for our participation.

Dr. Chris Bail, Duke University sociology professor and director of their Polarization Lab, recently published his research on political polarization in social media. A prevailing sentiment in our polarized political culture is that one way out of the divide is to break the echo chamber by exposing people to views from the other side of the political spectrum. This exposure is supposed to help broaden their perspective. His research found that the opposite occurred.

Those who stepped outside of their social media echo chambers were not humanizing others more. Instead, stepping outside served to sharpen the contrast between "us" and "them." Why is this?

Our focus upon Silicon Valley obscures a much more unsettling truth: the root source of political tribalism on social media lies deep inside ourselves. We think of platforms like Facebook and Twitter as places where we can seek information or entertain ourselves for a few minutes. But in an era of growing social isolation, social media platforms have become one of the most important tools we use to understand ourselves—and each other. We are addicted to social media not because it provides us with flashy eye candy or endless distractions, but because it helps us do something we humans are hardwired to do: present different versions of ourselves, observe what other people think of them, and revise our identities accordingly. But instead of a giant mirror that we can use to see our entire society, social media is more like a prism that refracts our identities—leaving us with a distorted understanding of each other, and ourselves.[5]

Social media addiction is related to our desire for control. We are enabled to present whatever view of ourselves we want. We can change that view based on how others respond to us. We can control the narrative we want to create about others, and it does not have to conform completely with reality or truth. In other words, our participation becomes identity forming for ourselves and the way that we perceive others.

Scroll through Twitter, YouTube, and Facebook. What do you find? "Representative Jane Destroys Liberal Representative Jessica!" "Congressman Michael Embarrasses Right Wing Congressman Justin!" The posts feed your disdain and contempt for the other side. Consider the impact this has on the church, whose identity is not to be shaped by partisan politics but by the Word of God. As Christians swim in these same waters, we are deceived into thinking that our participation is an exercise in controlling or promoting a righteous narrative.

Jesus' ministry is to do all for those he saves. This is how Paul could say, "Finally, be strong in the Lord and in the strength of his might" (Ephesians 6:10); or to Timothy, "You then, my child, be strengthened by the grace that is in Christ Jesus" (2 Timothy 2:1). This is how the Pastor can say, "Lift your drooping hands and strengthen your weak knees" (Hebrews

12:12). This is how Peter can say, "And after you have suffered a little while, the God of all grace, who has called you to his eternal glory in Christ, will himself restore, confirm, strengthen, and establish you" (1 Peter 5:10). The strength to endure through the fight is the fruit of Jesus' more excellent ministry, not only because he ministers in the true tabernacle, but also because he is the mediator of a better covenant.

BETTER COVENANT

The Pastor first mentions this better covenant in 7:22 when he says that God the Father swore to make Jesus the guarantor of a better covenant. He begins to flesh that out when he says that Christ has obtained a ministry that is much more excellent than the old as the covenant he mediates is better. Then he reminds them of God's promise to establish a new covenant through the prophet Jeremiah.

> For if that first covenant had been faultless, there would have been no occasion to look for a second. For he finds fault with them when he says: "Behold, the days are coming, declares the Lord, when I will establish a new covenant with the house of Israel and with the house of Judah, not like the covenant that I made with their fathers on the day when I took them by the hand to bring them out of the land of Egypt. For they did not continue in my covenant, and so I showed no concern for them, declares the Lord. For this is the covenant that I will make with the house of Israel after those days, declares the Lord: I will put my laws into their minds, and write them on their hearts, and I will be their God, and they shall be my people. And they shall not teach, each one his neighbor and each one his brother, saying, 'Know the Lord,' for they shall all know me, from the least of them to the greatest. For I will be merciful toward their iniquities, and I will remember their sins no more." (Hebrews 8:7-12)

Jeremiah ministered in the sixth century BC. He prophesied about the fall of Judah and the destruction of Jerusalem by the Babylonians.

The Lord said to Jeremiah, "I have appointed you this day to root up, to tear down, to destroy and to devastate, to build and to plant" (Jeremiah 1:10). Most of Jeremiah's message was harsh because God found fault with the people. The problem with that old covenant, that first covenant, was not that it was unholy or unrighteous, but that perfection could not be attained through it, as the Pastor has repeatedly demonstrated. Remember, God's goal for humanity is not "niceness"; it's perfection. And as the Pastor said in 7:19, the law made nothing perfect. The law reveals our sin, but it doesn't change our hearts.

The covenant established through Moses was temporary because it could not bring perfection. They should have known that because in Jeremiah's day a new and better covenant was promised. What's implied but unstated in 8:6 is that the covenant Jesus mediates is better, not only because it's established on better promises, but because Jesus is a better mediator. The Pastor doesn't have to say it here because he's already said it back in chapter 3.

> For Jesus has been counted worthy of more glory than Moses—as much more glory as the builder of a house has more honor than the house itself. (For every house is built by someone, but the builder of all things is God.) Now Moses was faithful in all God's house as a servant, to testify to the things that were to be spoken later, but Christ is faithful over God's house as a son. (Hebrews 3:3-6)

John puts it this way, "The law was given through Moses; grace and truth came through Jesus Christ" (John 1:17). That's a better deal. See, when the Pastor talks about a covenant, he's not talking about a mutual agreement or contract that needs an arbitrator to settle disputes. You hear about arbitration all the time in the sports world. A player wants more money, and the owner doesn't want to give him as much as he wants. So they bring in an arbitrator to settle the dispute based on the terms and conditions of the contract, and whatever the arbitrator decides is.

It's not like that with God's covenant. We're not negotiating with God such that we need a mediator to handle the negotiations. No, God sets the terms and conditions of the covenant, and they are not up for dispute. You might not like them, but they are settled. The mediator in God's covenant doesn't bring the two sides together to hammer out an agreement. Instead, the mediator speaks and acts with divine authority. The message of the covenant that came through Moses was basically this, "Do this and you will live" (Leviticus 18:5; Ezekiel 20:11).

Nobody could meet the conditions of that covenant. What makes Jesus the better mediator is that he came and met those conditions for us to the perfect letter of the law. He did it so that he could mediate the new covenant. His perfect obedience and his perfect sacrifice make him the only one who could guarantee the better covenant that Jeremiah spoke of six hundred years before Jesus came on the scene.

Again, God's goal for us is perfection because greater blessing is to draw near to him. The goal of the covenant is fellowship with God, a life of intimate fellowship in his presence. Jesus is a better mediator of a better covenant because he permanently secures our fellowship with God. Let's not get it twisted, however. Just because the covenant is new and better doesn't mean that it cannot be violated. I'm sorry to tell you, Christian—you and I are still covenant breakers. But having Jesus as our mediator, as our minister, as our high priest makes all the difference in the world. He has the power to secure permanent ongoing fellowship between us and God. That's the better life.

BETTER PROMISES

The first indication that this covenant is better is that it's not like the one he made with Israel in the exodus (Hebrews 8:9). Note that the Pastor isn't writing new Scripture here. He's quoting from a text that's over six hundred years old. He's saying that the time of this new covenant that Jeremiah prophesied about has come. Jeremiah's prophecy was necessary because there was a need for reconciliation. A divorce had taken place between God and his people, and it wasn't God's fault (Jeremiah 2:1-8). The Pastor says that there was occasion to look for a second covenant because God found fault with the people.

In Deuteronomy, Moses is giving the law to Israel a second time. In fact, that's what the title of the book means, second law. They Israelites are about to take possession of the Promised Land, and Moses is reminding them of their covenant with their God. Listen to this interaction between God and the people in Deuteronomy 5:26-29,

> "'For who is there of all flesh, that has heard the voice of the living God speaking out of the midst of fire as we have, and has still lived? Go near and hear all that the LORD our God will say and speak to us all that the LORD our God will speak to you, and we will hear and do it.' And the LORD heard your words, when you spoke to me. And the LORD said to me, 'I have heard the words of this people, which they have spoken to you. They are right in all that they have spoken. Oh that they had such a mind as this always, to fear me and to keep all my commandments, that it might go well with them and with their descendants forever!'"

In Deuteronomy 10:12-22, God says that he set his heart in love on their fathers and chose their offspring after them above all peoples. He commands them to "circumcise therefore the foreskin of your heart, and be no longer stubborn" (10:16). There, at the inauguration of the covenant, the problem is laid out.

After the Israelites took possession of the Promised Land, Joshua renewed the covenant with the people. He said to them,

> And if it is evil in your eyes to serve the LORD, choose this day whom you will serve, whether the gods your fathers served in the region beyond the River, or the gods of the Amorites in whose land you dwell. But as for me and my house, we will serve the LORD. (Joshua 24:15)

The people said, "We'll serve the Lord, for he is our God." What does Joshua say? "You are not able to serve the LORD, for he is a holy God. He is a jealous God" (24:18-19). The problem was evident from the very beginning. Despite their best intentions, the Israelites not only broke God's covenant, they ground it to dust.

Do you get it? When it comes to God, good intentions don't cut it. They had said repeatedly, "We'll serve the Lord!" But what they needed was a different heart. God has a dogged determination to make his people perfect, and he will not stop until he has accomplished his goal. As he said through Jeremiah and now through the Pastor, the day is coming when he will establish a new covenant with the house of Israel and the house of Judah. He has promised to take care of the reconciliation problem himself.

And the glory of this new covenant is that it goes beyond simply reconciling people to God. His powerful promise brings reconciliation both vertically and horizontally. The devastating effects of the demolition job they did on the covenant was a church split. The one nation of Israel split into Israel and Judah. Harmony turned into strife. Peace turned into discord and even hatred. Yet God continues to promise he will make a new covenant with the house of Israel and the house of Judah to take care of their reconciliation problem.

The promise of the reunion of Israel and Judah was symbolic of the healing of every human breach, and the reconciliation of all nations and persons in Christ points to the seed of Abraham in whom all the peoples of the earth are blessed and united (Galatians 3:8, 16, 27-29) because he "has broken down the dividing wall of hostility" (Ephesians 2:14). What God accomplishes through Christ is nothing less than the reconciliation of the world to himself (2 Corinthians 5:19).[6]

The promise of the new covenant is a promise to reconcile! God is going to once again be a husband to his people. He's going to bring all his people together into one redeemed humanity, a beautiful global community. What are the issues tempting you to neglect the fact that the Lord is in the business of reconciling us to one another? Reconciliation is impossible apart from Jesus Christ, but it is the expected way of life in the new covenant because of regeneration. God fixes our heart problem. He said in Deuteronomy 5:29, "Oh that they had such a heart as this always, to fear me, and keep all my commandments, that it might go well with them and their descendants forever!" That's the heart the Lord promises to give in the new covenant.

In Ezekiel 36:26-27 the Lord promises,

> I will give you a new heart, and a new spirit I will put within you. And I will remove the heart of stone from your flesh and give you a heart of flesh. And I will put my Spirit within you, and cause you to walk in my statutes and be careful to obey my rules.

In the new covenant, the Lord fixes the heart problem by replacing our hearts of stone with hearts of flesh. The law that Moses brought down from Mount Sinai on those tablets of stone could not penetrate the heart. Something different needed to take place, and it was never going to happen as long as keeping the law was an external matter only.

The stipulations and promises of both the old covenant and the new covenant are based on keeping the Law. Jesus said in Matthew 5:17, "Do not think that I have come to abolish the Law or the Prophets; I have not come to abolish them but to fulfill them." The new covenant is not called "new" because it contradicts the old. Jesus' words make it clear that both covenants demand obedience to the law. But the new covenant is not based on our obedience. It's based on the obedience of the Son of God.

Jesus obeyed the law of God perfectly, and because of that, when someone is united to Christ by faith, the law becomes an inside-out matter. The crazy thing about the new covenant is that obedience is promised! In the old covenant, God promised to be the Israelites' God on condition of their obedience. In the new covenant, because of the obedient one, Jesus Christ, God promises to put his law on our minds and write it on our hearts. The result of regeneration is that you will open this Word and you will find delight in following what God says. You will find encouragement in his promises. You will be glad for him to correct you because what you will want is to do all for him.

In 2 Corinthians 3, the apostle Paul provides a parallel promise to Hebrews 8. Here's how he describes what happens to those who receive this heart transplant from God, "We all, with unveiled faces, are looking as in a mirror at the glory of the Lord and are being transformed into the same image from glory to glory; this is from the Lord who is the Spirit" (2 Corinthians 3:18 CSB). Remember, the goal that the Pastor has been emphasizing is perfection, and the Spirit of God, through the Word of God, regenerates hearts and transforms people into the same glorious image we see of Jesus Christ in the pages of Scripture.

In this case, new is definitely better! Christian hope becomes inextinguishable because the better hope is secured by a better priest who ministers as mediator of a better covenant with better promises. This is the point the Pastor has built from Hebrews 5:1–10:18. The meat of his exhortation has been doctrine dominant, driving home the message that this is what we are to believe about Jesus Christ. He is a high priest after the order of Melchizedek. Therefore, he holds his priesthood for all time. Unlike the priests of old, he made one all-sufficient offering for sin, securing an eternal redemption. He has permanently cleansed his people. This is what he's doing for you now. He lives to make intercession for his people, appearing now in the presence of God the Father on our behalf. The old covenant is done away with. He has abolished the old to establish the new.

In the next section, the Pastor will get practical. Having explained what his readers ought to know, he will turn to discussing how they ought to live. In other words, this good doctrine and instruction is for living. It's not just for meditation, but it serves as the foundation for how the Christian life is lived in hope, specifically in community with others rather than isolation, holding fast the confession of our hope without wavering as we stir one another up to love and good works (Hebrews 10:23-24).

PART 3

IN NEED OF ENDURANCE

7

REMEMBER TO ENDURE

It is God, not human beings, who will have the last word.
God's final triumph over evil does not depend on our success
in overcoming sin and death; if it did, we would truly
have no hope. . . . The way of Christian community is not,
however, to retreat from horror into the solace of personal
religion, but to proclaim Christ's hope to the world (the
not-yet in the now) by involving ourselves in . . ."strategies
of hope," like the ministries being carried out in this parish
and Christian communities around the world even now.

FLEMING RUTLEDGE, *ADVENT*

"Glory be to God for dappled things," wrote Gerard Manley Hopkins in his poem "Pied Beauty."[1] To be "dappled" is to be variegated, exhibiting different colors. Hopkins glorifies God in his poem for the skies, fish, finches, landscapes, and the like. All the created variety in this world points to the glory and grandeur of God.

Our God loves difference. He is the author of dappled things—he "fathers-forth," as Hopkins puts it. He spoke the delightful benediction "very good" over the beautifully diverse creation at the end of the sixth day. It is no minor point that humanity crowns the creation account in Genesis 1. All beauty in creation has God as its source, but humanity was destined for what I call beautiful community. As Father, Son, and Holy

Spirit, God is the beautiful one who has brought copies of himself into being. And yet, because of sin, we cannot pursue beautiful community, unity in diversity, without engaging the issues of injustice and oppression.

This engagement has become fraught with new and intensified difficulty for the church in the United States since the murders of George Floyd, Ahmaud Arbery, and Breonna Taylor in 2020. My work puts me in constant conversation with pastors and ministry leaders who are trying to faithfully navigate the intense debate around race and justice. They have a particular intent to lead their churches into a more robust pursuit of unity in diversity, and without fail, they will describe what I call "the vise effect."

Some congregants with a high degree of excitement and impatience respond to this leadership with sentiments like, "It's about time that we're addressing the problem of race and justice in the church and society! How can we expect to truly love and welcome our diverse neighbors if we do not engage the issues that are affecting their lives?" Another contingent of congregants are pushing from the other end. "Wait a minute!" they say. "This feels like we're buying into the culture's narrative on these issues. Slow down. Let's make sure that our church is not forsaking the gospel for social relevance."

Church leaders are caught in this vise and many wonder whether they ought to go back to the good old days of ignoring these topics altogether. Of course, it's a myth to refer to the days of proclaiming a gospel that does not deal forthrightly with the sin of racial injustice as "good." A non-truncated gospel proclamation engages the most difficult issues of the day while calling us to the embodied hope of unity in diversity. Let me explain what I mean.

My grandmother left Wilmington, North Carolina, for Harlem in 1947, leaving her six children behind for an extended time. She wanted to provide a better life for them and the generations that would come after—a better life in the form of opportunities to pursue higher education and employment opportunities so that her posterity would not be burdened with poverty. In 1952, my mother followed her. She wanted to be a nurse from as far back as she could remember and knew there was no way for her to achieve that dream in Wilmington. So she followed Nana to New York and accomplished her goal. The two of them were a part of the Great American Migration, the mass exodus of African Americans out of the southern states from 1900–1970. I sat with my mother back in 2014 to record her story for my posterity.

In January 2020 I was preparing for a ministry trip to Wilmington and had just finished reading the book *Wilmington's Lie: The Murderous Coup of 1898 and the Rise of White Supremacy*, which details the tragic, hostile coup of the city government in November 1898. Today, a landmark stands at the site where the white mob gathered, acknowledging that the violence left untold numbers of African Americans dead while overthrowing the city government and installing the coup leader as mayor. What was the reason for the takeover? A flourishing Black community in a city that was becoming a post–Civil War model for Black and white cooperation.

In the lead up to the coup, Rev. Peyton Hoge, pastor of First Presbyterian Church in Wilmington, preached white supremacist messages to his congregation. Other white ministers joined in, all at the request of Democratic politicians. On the Sunday following the coup, Rev. James W. Kramer of Brooklyn Baptist Church in Wilmington declared to his congregation, "God from the beginning of time intended that intelligent white men should lead the people and rule the country."[2] Rev. Hoge himself carried around a Winchester rifle during the overthrow.

Today we say that politics has no place in the pulpit, but Rev. Kramer said in his post-coup sermon, "I believe that the whites were doing God's services, as the results for good have been felt in businesses, in politics and in the church. We will give the negro justice and will treat him kindly, but never again will we be ruled by him."[3] On the Sunday after the coup, Rev. Hoge opened his sermon saying, "Since we last met in these walls, we have taken a city."[4]

Why bring up this tragic event from 1898? Two reasons: first, there is a direct connection between the coup and the lack of opportunity for my mother in the 1940s and '50s. The coup set the city on a course from which it has not yet recovered. In 1898, Wilmington's population was 56 percent Black. Today it is less than 20 percent Black. Following the coup, a Black person was not elected to city office again until 1972. The white church was more than complicit in the coup, as white ministers actively supported it. We cannot effectively promote a vision for the beautiful community God desires to cultivate without bringing to the surface the real-life dehumanizing and oppressive conditions that have contributed to the ongoing racial and political divides we experience in the church today.

The second reason I mention the coup is that during my 2020 visit to Wilmington, prior to the pandemic shut down, I met and interacted with a racially and denominationally diverse coalition of pastors who are striving to bear witness in the city of our unity in Jesus Christ. For them and the city, the coup is not ancient history. It still casts a shadow over the church. They know that they must engage the lasting effects of this historical event if they are to experience the intimate communion the Scriptures describe for God's people.

You see, it's easy for us to condemn the overt systemic racism at work in the coup of 1898. It's much more difficult for us to identify in the present what informs our responses to the polarizing issues of our own day. Given the difficulty, is it worth it—or even possible—to press through the polarization?

Here is another truth, and this one is glorious: beautiful community is already a reality. The redemption of the world has been accomplished by the victory of God in the crucifixion of Jesus Christ. "It is finished," our Lord said as he hung on the cross (John 19:30), and he was vindicated by the Spirit when he rose from the dead (1 Timothy 3:16). The church is called to be a sign of unity for the human race that will one day be perfectly achieved. We participate in the visible communion of the church through our membership in a local congregation.

This means that beautiful community primarily plays out in the context of the local church. It is demonstrated by the gathering of people from diverse backgrounds, cultures, ethnicities, political persuasions, abilities, and social statuses into a loving, persevering community. God is going to knit humanity back together in his Son. It is going to happen as sure as night follows day. The question is what will enable us to endure in hope committing to the pursuit of beautiful community while seeking the unity of the Spirit across lines of difference?

By definition, a Christian is a member of a family—a spiritual family. Living out the Christian faith is done with one another, and the Pastor begins to press his readers on this reality as he transitions from his primary focus on doctrinal statements to exhortations for living. But first, he summarizes everything he's said previously in two verses.

> Therefore, brothers, since we have confidence to enter the holy places by the blood of Jesus, by the new and living way that he opened for us through the curtain, that is, through his flesh, and since we have a great priest over the house of God. (Hebrews 10:19-21)

The old way into the earthly sanctuary was just a copy of the heavenly sanctuary. It had limited access. The veil in the tabernacle excluded the people from the most holy place where the glory of the Lord rested above the mercy seat. But in Jesus there is a new veil, his body, and it is a door through which everyone who follows him has free and unlimited access to God. The way is "new" because Jesus inaugurated the new covenant, doing away with the old. It will remain new because, unlike the old, it will never become obsolete. It's a "living way" because, unlike the priests of old, Jesus didn't offer the blood of dead animals. He offered up himself on the cross, and then he rose bodily from the grave, ascended into heaven, and entered into the heavenly sanctuary once for all by means of his own blood.

Jesus has provided a new and living way for the people of God. We have a great high priest over the house of God. Therefore, we can have confidence, and it is out of that confidence that the Pastor begins to call his readers to some "let us" exhortations.

UPWARD CONFIDENCE

Because of the confidence Christ followers have been given to enter the heavenly sanctuary, the Pastor charges his readers, "Let us draw near with a true heart in full assurance of faith because we have had our hearts sprinkled clean from an evil conscience and our body has been washed with pure water" (Hebrews 10:22, author's translation). Let us draw near to what? Or to whom? The first time he used this phrase was in 4:16 where he said, "Let us then with confidence draw near to the throne of grace, that we may receive mercy and find grace to help in time of need." In that case, the call is to a heavenly confidence reflected in our prayer life. Take advantage of what you have, Christian. Jesus has provided what no one else could, so his people have what no one else has, namely, free access to God.

In Jesus, by his blood, we enter heaven itself, into the very presence of God.

> But you have come to Mount Zion and to the city of the living God, the heavenly Jerusalem, and to innumerable angels in festal gathering, and to the assembly of the firstborn who are enrolled in heaven, and to God, the judge of all, and to the spirits of the righteous made perfect, and to Jesus, the mediator of a new covenant, and to the sprinkled blood that speaks a better word than the blood of Abel. (Hebrews 12:22-24)

The Pastor doesn't say that you're going to Mount Zion, or that you'll come to the city of the living God eventually. You cannot see it with your eyes, but right now you have already come to God. Therefore, let us draw near to him with a true heart in full assurance of faith.

A true heart is one that has been changed by the Spirit of God through faith in Jesus. And when we come to him with that kind of heart, we don't come timidly or sheepishly as if we're afraid God isn't going to hear us. Drawing near to God with a true heart means understanding that you're not talking to a wall. Our Father in heaven doesn't have an anger management problem nor does he make empty promises. There's nothing wrong with his hearing, and he loves to answer the prayers of his children. That's why the Pastor says to draw near with a true heart in "full assurance of faith." Be fully assured that God hears and answers his children.

The Pastor emphasizes that we can have this upward confidence because we're clean inside and out. Our hearts have been sprinkled clean from an evil conscience and our bodies have been washed with pure water. His readers were converted to Christianity out of Judaism. They would've been concerned about ritual purity. In 9:19, he mentioned how the first covenant was inaugurated with blood. Moses sprinkled the book and the people with blood, and there was a basin with water for the priests to wash before they entered their service. However, none of those rituals could cleanse the conscience or change the condition of a person's heart. But the blood of Jesus has cleansed your conscience, and the Holy Spirit has provided spiritual renewal such that you are clean inside and outside.

It doesn't matter whether you're well-groomed or haven't bathed in a week—there is no concern for the Christian when it comes to ritual impurity and our ability to stand before God. Because Jesus makes us clean, we have fellowship with God and we live out the faith by drawing near to him repeatedly.

INWARD CONFESSION

Following this call to an upward confidence, the Pastor writes that Christians ought to also have an inward confession. "Let us hold fast the confession of our hope without wavering, for he who promised is faithful" (10:23). By phrasing it this way, I don't mean that he's encouraging "confessing to yourself." Rather, the upward exhortation, the confidence to draw close to God in prayer and worship, is followed by an inward exhortation to hold fast to the confession of our *hope*. That's an inward experience.

And we should not be surprised by his phrasing here as he has used it repeatedly throughout the letter.

- "But Christ is faithful over God's house as a son. And we are his house if indeed we hold fast our confidence and our boasting in our hope" (Hebrews 3:6).

- "Since then we have a great high priest who has passed through the heavens, Jesus, the Son of God, let us hold fast our confession" (Hebrews 4:14).

- "And we desire each one of you to show the same earnestness [that you've shown for God's name in serving the saints] to have the full assurance of hope until the end" (Hebrews 6:11).

- "So when God desired to show more convincingly to the heirs of the promise the unchangeable character of his purpose, he guaranteed it with an oath, so that by two unchangeable things, in which it is impossible for God to lie, we who have fled for refuge might have strong encouragement to hold fast to the hope set before us" (Hebrews 6:17-18).

The confession of our hope is that Jesus Christ is Lord and is faithful to fulfill every promise. The apostle Peter says that we have been "born again to a living hope through the resurrection of Jesus Christ from the dead" (1 Peter 1:3). By his resurrection, Jesus is confirmed Lord over all. As we have already said in several ways, Christian hope is substantive, not superstitious. It's not wishful thinking. The Christian hope is a hope for living.

Once again, the Pastor is urging his readers to hold on to it. Don't let it go. Then he tells them to hold fast to it without wavering. The Christian hope is a sure and steadfast anchor for the soul. And this is the connection—living out the faith by drawing near to God in prayer and worship strengthens us to hold on inwardly to the confession of our hope because we become more and more assured that God, who made the promise, is faithful.

We cannot afford to forget that this letter's original audience is going through adversity. They're facing persecution and hardship because they believe in Jesus. Nothing tests our faith in Jesus like adversity. The temptation is to compromise what we believe about Jesus just a little bit because things might get better. The Pastor says, "This thing has got to be way down deep on the inside. It's got to be so deep in you that you hold tightly without wavering through the storm."

This is strong language. It's like when you watch college football, and it is neck and neck. Who's going to come out on top? The referee blows the whistle at the end of the third quarter, and the camera pans over to the sideline and all the players are raising four fingers in the air. Fourth quarter. Time to step it up and dig in till the end.

That's the sense here. Hold on to the end. The end of the ages has been inaugurated with the coming of Jesus. Hold on to that confession of hope. Step it up and dig in till the end.

OUTWARD COMMITMENT

The evidence of this holding fast inwardly without wavering is an outward commitment to one another seen within the church. This is not a private deal where you can have your private meditative prayer life and feel assured about your faith then go on and live your life until you get to heaven. No, living out the faith is messy business because it involves my ongoing commitment to others within the body of Christ, *especially* when there is great difficulty.

"And let us consider how to stir up one another to love and good works, not neglecting to meet together, as is the habit of some, but encouraging one another, and all the more as you see the Day drawing near" (Hebrews 10:24-25). The last time he used that verb *consider* was in 3:1 when he said, "Therefore, holy brothers and sisters, you who share in a heavenly calling, consider Jesus, the apostle and high priest of our confession."

To consider Jesus is not to weigh whether following Jesus or believing in him is worth it. To consider Jesus means fixing our thoughts and attention on him. With that in mind, the exhortation here is for us to be concerned about one another. Let us consider one another. Let us fix our thoughts on one another. Living out the faith is messy business because, by necessity, it involves an outward commitment to be intimately involved with one another. There is no other conclusion to draw from if Christians are to stir up one another to love and good works.

The Pastor is saying that within the body of Christ, we should have our thoughts so fixed on one another that we are moved to provoke one another toward love and good works. You cannot do that with folks you do not know. You have no credibility with people you don't know.

As a part of the church, we get to know and are known by one another, in part, so that we can incite one another to love and good works. People attend a church and join for a variety of reasons—the music, preaching, programs they offer, and so on. How often does what the Pastor say here make the list? I want to be at a place where people are going to keep me accountable, where I will not be allowed to sit on the sidelines. I want to be at a place where people are not going to be content to let me dip in and dip out when I feel like it. I want to be at a place where people are not going to let me just play church. I want to be connected to sisters and brothers in Christ who will not shy away from loving engagement of the issues that may threaten to divide. I submit to you that these desires do not make the list very often. But the biblical truth is that the Christian life is a "one another" life.

Apparently, dipping in and dipping out because things got a little rough was a problem for the readers of the Pastor's letter. He tells them in 10:25 that part of getting in one another's business by stirring one another up to love and good works is not neglecting to meet, like some of them were doing. We're no different. When things get rough, we're tempted to check out for a minute. And the Pastor is saying, "Are you serious? Given all that you know about Jesus, who he is, what he's done, what he's doing now, who you are in him, you're letting adversity keep you away from the place where hope and encouragement is found? Are you out of your mind?" This is not simply about gathering for worship on the Lord's Day. It includes that, for sure, but the focus of gathering is to live out the faith as a life commitment.

The evidence of your upward confidence in fellowship with God and your inward fastening to the confession of hope is the outward commitment to the local body, meaning the people. If that isn't present, the other two are suspect as well. Our faith in God takes us up to heaven for ongoing fellowship and worship in his presence. Our hope in him and his promise anchors us and enables us not to waver. Then our love for God and one another moves us to stir one another up toward encouragement. Faith, hope, and love. As messy as it is, that is what the church is called to.

"Remember to endure"—that's the Pastor's message. His readers are to continue in hope with an upward confidence, inward confession, and outward commitment, remembering that they've been through adversity in the past. They're facing adversity now, but it's not new. Just like they were able to press through adversity before, they needed to press through it again. What does remembering look like? The end of chapter 10 lays out three practical facets.

ENDURE WITH JOY

To help his readers deal with their current situation, the Pastor takes them back in time. He warns them with hard words in 10:26-31 about the terrible fate of those who reject the Son of God. Now he wants to let them know they aren't going to go in that direction. The evidence of that, he says, is the way they were able to endure through extreme suffering and even have joy in the middle of it.

What he calls them to remember in 10:32-34 is something that more would prefer to forget.

> But remember the former days, in which, after you were enlightened,
> you endured an extensive struggle with sufferings. This included
> insults and also persecutions as you were sometimes made a public

spectacle. At other times you became partners with those who were so treated. For you sympathized with the prisoners and you willingly received the seizure of your possessions with joy because you knew you yourselves had a better and lasting possession. (Hebrews 10:32-34, author's translation)

To paraphrase, he's saying—after God the Father qualified you to share in the inheritance of the saints in light by transferring you out of the domain of darkness into the kingdom of his beloved Son (Colossians 1:12-13), remember what happened? After the light came on and you repented of your sins, trusting in Jesus Christ as your God and Savior, all hell broke loose in your life. Remember how you had to endure a hard struggle with sufferings!

That doesn't sound right. That sounds backward. We prefer the opposite plot, that times become so much better after putting our faith in Christ. But that's not what the Pastor says. He doesn't try to motivate them by sugarcoating the truth. Neither did Jesus. He told his disciples, "If anyone would come after me, let him deny himself and take up his cross daily and follow me" (Luke 9:23).

The Pastor reminds his readers that they are doing just that. They followed Christ by enduring, by standing their ground without wavering even when made a public spectacle through insults and persecution. They weren't ashamed to let people know that other Christians who were being thrown in prison were your brothers and sisters. Having compassion on prisoners was dangerous during that time because it meant supplying them with food, water, and clothing so that they wouldn't die. They paid a heavy price for their compassion.

Here's where we object. This can't be right. Hebrews 10:34 must be a typo. The Pastor commends them not only for enduring, but also for not moaning and groaning about their suffering. In fact, he notes they accepted the plundering of their property with *joy*!

It's likely that most people do not want to be possessed by their possessions. People who take life seriously typically do not want to be controlled by material things. In some ways, having a loose grip on our possessions is a virtue in our society. I might be willing to risk my possessions to help fund a new business venture. People take out a second mortgage on their home or liquidate their retirement savings for these kinds of things. While I do not want to be controlled by material things, there's a difference between willingly risking my stuff and having my stuff taken away from me.

A few years ago, we transitioned from suburban life back into city life. My wife and I moved from Brooklyn to the Washington, DC, metropolitan area in the midnineties. We spent twenty years raising our children in the suburbs between DC and Baltimore. After those two decades, we moved into DC for a new ministry job and were happy to be urbanites again. Our youngest child was in middle school and about to experience city living during his formative adolescent years. One evening over dinner, Kim and I were reminiscing about growing up in Brooklyn. I began to share the joys of growing up in the city, but also shared some of my challenging experiences. I vividly recalled the three times I was robbed.

The first time, I was around eight years old, riding my bike outside while my father was washing the car. My mother gave me strict instruction not to ride around the corner where I couldn't be seen. Dad wasn't as strict, so I decided to ask him if I could go around the corner, and he said yes. Children always know which parent to ask for what they want. As I happily rode around the corner, he went inside for more cleaning supplies. Before I knew it, a much older boy stood in front of me and asked if he could ride my bike. I let him hop on, and off he went. Bye-bye bike.

The second occurrence was several years later while in upper elementary school. I was excited because we were going to make crepes in school that day. It was rare that I carried any money on me, but I had a few dollars because students were asked to contribute to the cost of the food. During those days, elementary school students were given passes that enabled them to ride the bus or train for free. While waiting at the bus stop, I was approached by three older boys. I couldn't tell you how old they were. I just know that I had to look up at them. "You have any money?" "No," I replied, fully aware of the few dollars in my pocket. I took out the little fold I used to hold my bus pass to show that there was no money in it. Off they went with my bus pass. Embarrassed and dejected, I walked to school and arrived very late. No cell phones in those days meant that my parents were worried sick, not knowing where I was when the school called.

Robbery number three will have a familiar ring. It was one week after my fourteenth birthday. My parents gave me a new twelve-speed bike. Fridays were when we got Chinese food from the restaurant a block away on Flatbush Avenue. My cousin and I were tasked with picking up the order. My mother said to us, "Don't ride your bikes. Walk." My cousin and I decided to disobey her command. As we waited for the order, our bikes leaned against the window inside of the restaurant, three guys walked by outside. I heard one say, "Yo! Bikes!" They kept walking, but I had an uneasy feeling in my gut. Once we grabbed our order, we headed out of the restaurant, bags in hand full of Friday night dinner. We hadn't pedaled more than a few feet into the street before those three rushed us. Two came around me and demanded that I get off the bike. The third rushed my cousin with the same demand. We got off and handed over the bikes. Not so ironically, we ended up walking. I'll spare you the details of my mother's response.

I was sort of in my own world as I retold these stories of Brooklyn life in the 1970s and '80s to Kim and my son at dinner. I was snapped out of that walk down memory lane when I looked at my son. He was crying! My stories made him afraid to move into the city. Feeling horrible, I reassured him that this was not going to be his experience. And it hasn't been. It also helped that he'd been training in Krav Maga for years and became an instructor at sixteen years old.

What were his tears about? They weren't just about the threat of bodily harm. They were about the threat of people taking what belongs to us. When our things are taken away from us, we feel violated. We experience a lot of emotions, but joy isn't one of them. Joy was nowhere to be found for me during or after any of those incidents. It would be odd to have my possessions taken and instead of feeling depressed, embarrassed, angry, despondent, or sad, feel joy. How amazing it is, then, that the Pastor reminds them they received the plundering of their possessions with joy because they knew they had a *better* and more lasting possession. And what was that better possession? It was their eternal inheritance in Jesus Christ. The gospel message is radical. By convincing us that possessing life in Jesus is better than possessing anything else, we joyfully embrace loss for the sake of the gospel.

We should not assume that the Pastor's readers were happy about having their possessions taken by force. It's likely they experienced anger, sadness, and maybe even a desire for revenge! But those things were not primary for them. Fleming Rutledge wrote,

> God's final triumph over evil does not depend on our success in overcoming sin and death; if it did, we would truly have no hope. . . . The way of Christian community is not, however, to retreat from horror into the solace of personal religion, but to proclaim Christ's hope to the world (the not-yet in the now) by involving ourselves in . . . "strategies of hope."

Frustrations arise for us, and we are tempted to fall into hopelessness regarding Christianity and Christians because we often have a different understanding of what successful Christian ministry looks like. Rutledge is correct. The triumph over evil that was accomplished by God in the cross of Jesus Christ will one day be fully realized in time and space and evident to all creation. We have to remember that this triumph includes God's victory over *our* sin and evil to make us citizens of his kingdom. The only thing we contributed to that victory was the sin and evil. The victory didn't depend on our successfully overcoming sin in our lives, and his victory over the depravity of our world doesn't depend on us either. That means success may look like failure and loss.

The readers of Hebrews were struggling, and the call was for them to remember the joy they experienced in loss! The implication is that they aren't responding to the current struggle with that same joy. Previously, they had not retreated into the solace of personal religion. They were public with their faith and affiliation to Jesus, and it resulted in suffering. The exhortation is here because there's no guarantee that the sufferings of this world will be met with joy over the better possession we have in Christ.

ENDURE BY NEED

It is hard, particularly in our culture, to have a tangible sense of the value of what it means to possess life in Christ. That difficulty is why the Pastor doesn't just remind his readers of their joyful endurance in the past, but he uses the memory to point them to the need they have to continue enduring.

He moves from enduring with joy to enduring by need. "Therefore do not throw away your confidence, which has a great reward. For you have need of endurance, so that when you have done the will of God you may receive what is promised" (Hebrews 10:35-36). In the middle of difficulty and struggles, spiritual realities can seem so distant. That eternal inheritance that Jesus secured when he rose from the dead seems like something that's far away. And because we still have to wait for what we know to be true by faith to become true by sight, we're pulled toward what we can see with our eyes.

The readers of Hebrews were being pulled back toward the old system of temple worship and sacrifice that had been done away with. But it was what they could see and touch. That pull toward putting our hopes in things we see with our eyes and touch with our hands is like a tractor beam in sci-fi movies that imprisons other ships, preventing their escape.

But the Pastor's message is that if you're a Christian, there's another tractor beam at work, pulling you away from the things of this life that so easily ensnare you and turn your focus away from the Lord. That tractor beam is the confidence he's talking about in 10:35. It's that same confidence he's written about repeatedly, the one that permits us to draw near to the throne of grace (4:16) and enter into the heavenly sanctuary by the blood of Jesus with a true heart in full assurance of faith (10:19).

Jesus has opened the new and living way into the presence of God through his body, and the heavenly tractor beam continues to pull us to him. The confidence he gives us to draw near is stronger than the pull to turn away from him and be satisfied with anything less than the great reward the Pastor is talking about. This confidence to continue drawing near to God will ensure the endurance, the staying power needed to persevere in this life.

Endurance is "faithful perseverance under and in the face of pressure and suffering and discouragement of every kind."[5] Do we have a sense of the absolute need to persevere under and in the face of pressure and suffering and discouragement of every kind? We would rather not have to deal with pressure. We would prefer to avoid suffering and discouragement. But none of us get to live in this world without having to deal with pressure, suffering, and discouragement. If we must deal with them, what are we going to do with them? Are we going to try and fill our lives with so much fun that we entertain them away? Are we going to try and fill our lives with so much work that we're too busy to be discouraged? Are we going to try and medicate them away? Are we going to try and drink them away, or whatever else might help us deal?

The Bible says that what we need is *endurance through it*. And the image the Pastor presents is that of enduring with joy. The need to endure is only met as we draw near to the throne of grace with confidence. What we receive is the type of assurance of hope that brings joy to the heart even though we're not happy about our struggles or the disappointments we face from ourselves, our brothers and sisters in Christ, our neighbors, and our society.

The Pastor says, you have *need* of endurance so that when you have done the will of God you may receive what is promised. What's the will of God? That we endure! God's will is that his people stand firm to the end. He wants you to persevere through the hardship in Christian community. He wants you to trust him. He wants you to say, "Lord, your grace is sufficient for me, even in this." We need to endure because endurance is ultimately what distinguishes us as belonging to Jesus Christ.

ENDURE BY FAITH

The need to endure is a spiritual responsibility, but just like everything else in the Christian life, God doesn't leave us on our own. Jesus says of his disciples, "Apart from me you can do nothing" (John 15:5). Paul puts it this way, "I can do all things through him who strengthens me" (Philippians 4:13). So the Pastor lets us know in 10:37-39 that endurance is by faith in Jesus Christ. He gives a short citation from Isaiah 26:20, then quotes from Habakkuk 2:3-4 when he says,

> For yet a very little while he who is coming will come and he will not delay. But my righteous one will live by faith, and if he turns back, my soul does not delight in him. But we do not belong to those who turn back into destruction, but we belong to those of faith who preserve their soul. (Hebrews 10:37-39, author's translation)

If you're going to endure, there's only one way to live—by faith in Jesus Christ. What does that faith look like? It believes that Jesus, the coming one, will not delay in fulfilling God's saving plan. It has such a trust in God's promise and in his Word that it refuses to turn back and is determined to persevere. To turn back is to renounce the life of faith because you think that something else is better or easier.

The Pastor says, "We're not like that! I've seen the evidence of your faith. I know what type of people you are. We're not like people who shrink back because we think there's something out there better than Jesus. We're not like those folks who shrink back and are destroyed. We belong to the group of people who have faith and preserve their souls." He is about to go into great detail in chapter 11 about this "soul preserving faith." He's starting to let them know that they are in a long line of faithful ones who don't turn back from their faith, from their confidence to approach the throne of grace, from the assurance of their hope, but who endure through trouble to the end.

Remember to endure. Remember that the Christian life isn't a sprint. It's a marathon. Remember that God gives grace and power to endure hardships and disappointments with joy. Remember that to be a Christian means to have need of endurance. Remember that enduring through life with joy is by faith in the risen Savior. And most of all, remember "Jesus, the founder and perfecter of our faith, who for the joy that was set before him endured the cross, despising the shame, and is seated at the right hand of the throne of God" (Hebrews 12:1-3).

8

PERSEVERE BY FAITH

If you can dream—and not make dreams your master;
If you can think—and not make thoughts your aim;
If you can meet with Triumph and Disaster
And treat those two impostors just the same;
If you can bear to hear the truths you've spoken
Twisted by knaves to make a trap for fools,
Or watch the things you gave your life to, broken,
And stoop and build 'em up with worn-out tools.

RUDYARD KIPLING, "IF—"

In 2018 students at the University of Manchester in England painted over the mural of a poem by Rudyard Kipling in the university's newly refurbished students' union. They replaced it with the poem "Still I Rise" by Maya Angelou. An article about the incident notes that the union's liberation and access officer, Sarah Kahn, said in a statement on Facebook that students had not been consulted about the art that would decorate the union building. "We, as an exec team, believe that Kipling stands for the opposite of liberation, empowerment and human rights—the things that we, as an SU, stand for," she said.[1]

Kipling is the author of the poem "The White Man's Burden," which was written to encourage the United States to assume colonial control of the Philippines. But that isn't the poem that was put up in the new students' center. The poem they painted over was another famous Kipling poem called "If—."

"If—" was one of my father's favorite poems. I never asked him why, but he had learned it in school growing up in Trinidad when that country was still a British colony. The poem is written from the perspective of a father to his son. The father is imparting some wise words of advice about growing into manhood. Indeed, the last lines of the poem are,

> If you can fill the unforgiving minute
>> With sixty seconds worth of distance run
> Yours is the Earth and everything that's in it,
>> And—which is more—you'll be a Man, my son![2]

These words are worth talking about by themselves, but our focus on the link between hope and faith brings to my mind a different portion of the poem. In the second stanza, Kipling says,

> If you can dream—and not make dreams your master;
>> If you can think—and not make thoughts your aim;
> If you can meet with Triumph and Disaster
>> And treat those two impostors just the same;
> If you can bear to hear the truths you've spoken
>> Twisted by knaves to make a trap for fools,
> Or watch the things you gave your life to broken,
>> And stoop and build 'em up with worn-out tools.[3]

The father is telling his son he has to get up and do something. It's cool to dream, but dreams can't be your master. It's cool to think, but thoughts can't be your aim. And the third line is the reality check. When you get up and do something, you're going to meet with both triumph and disaster, so you've got to treat those two impostors just the same. Don't get too high with the triumphs or too low when disaster hits. He's saying, "Son, if you're going to become a man you've got to have the right perspective on both success and suffering."

That's a picture similar to what the Pastor paints for us in what may be the most famous chapter in Hebrews. He gives them a history lesson on what it looks like for Christians to persevere by faith. Faith perseveres by seeing the unseen. Faith perseveres by obeying God's Word. Faith perseveres by holding tightly to God's promises. He emphatically demonstrates that faith can persevere well through both triumph and disaster. Hebrews 11 is full of examples of God's people who by faith experienced both impossible success and impossible suffering.

The Pastor instructs us on how to have the right perspective when it comes to success and suffering. The perspective is this: the life of faith in Christ involves both. Dad might not like me modifying Kipling's poem, but "if you can meet with Triumph and Disaster, and understand that *God* is still the same"—then you're persevering by faith.

In this chapter, we will dive into Hebrews 11 to find out that persevering by faith means having x-ray vision, living for the city, and facing the impossible.

X-RAY VISION

I can't talk about x-ray vision without referencing Superman. Everyone knows it is one of his powers, and the internet is full of theories about how it works. Inquiring minds want to know whether Superman's x-ray vision can cause cancer! If you've ever had x-rays taken of your teeth during a dental procedure, you can understand the concern. You're lying in the chair, and the dental assistant puts a lead apron over your chest. Then they stick that uncomfortable device in your mouth and tell you to bite down while lining up the machine right at the spot they want to image. What do they do next? They leave the room before they turn it on!

So it's a legitimate question whether Superman's x-ray vision can cause cancer when he looks through people. Now, if the *ScienceBlogs* is correct, you and I may not need to worry if Superman shows up and peers into our insides. One writer says,

Superman is seeing the subtle energy fields involved in the inter-transformation of energy into matter. His ability to distinguish those fields depends upon the "signal-to-noise ratio" between any object he is sensing and any intervening objects.[4]

You wouldn't get cancer from Superman's eyes because he is *perceiving* the x-rays that are always present and passing through your body rather than projecting them at you, bouncing them off something behind you, and back through your body.

I have no idea whether this is correct, but the idea of Superman *perceiving* or *seeing* what is already there is exactly on point with what the Pastor is emphasizing as he begins this "hall of faith" chapter of Hebrews 11. The questions he aims to answer are what is faith and what does it mean to live by faith? The first three words of Hebrews 11 are "Now faith *is*."

A lot of folks define faith as wishful thinking. It's just hoping that things are going to work out well even though you're not sure. When the Bible talks about faith (or hope, for that matter), it never presents faith as wishful thinking, or a wish for something better. Even if we say, "I know the Bible does not talk about faith as a wish or a fantasy," our lives will often declare the opposite. We struggle to believe that what the Bible says is true because every one of us would rather live by sight than live by faith. We can put the spiritual realities in the fantasy compartment of our brains because it's hard to be confident in the fact that the heavenly realities the Bible gives us are more real than what we experience with our five senses.

Hebrews 11 begins by describing our need to have eyes that are sensitive enough to perceive the truth despite what things appear to be. Like Superman, we need to perceive what's really going on, even though it's unseen. The Pastor helps us take faith in God and his promises out of the fantasy department and into the firm position of the realist reality. He wants his congregation to know the blessing of enduring through life by faith, and the first seven verses of chapter 11 point us in that direction.

What faith sees. I didn't bring up x-ray vision because I wanted to talk about Superman. I did it because of the connection between sight and faith that brackets the first seven verses of Hebrews 11. Faith in the unseen undergirds the message of the whole chapter, but it's of specific note in verses 1-3 and 7.

> Now faith is the assurance of what we hope for. It is the conviction about the things we don't *see*. For by it the people of old received their commendation. By faith we understand that the universe was created by God's utterance, such that what is *seen* did not come to be from the things that are *visible*. . . . By faith Noah, after he was warned about the things that were not yet ***seen***, because he was devout he built an ark in order to save his household. Through this salvation he condemned the world and became an heir of the righteousness that corresponds to faith. (Hebrews 11:1-3, 7, author's translation)

Back in 2010 a new version of the movie *The Karate Kid* hit the screens. Twelve-year-old Dre moves with his mom from Detroit to China, and things do not go well for him. Once, when Dre has just gotten beat up by the bad kids, Mr. Han jumps in and saves him. After he chases the kids off, Mr. Han returns to take care of Dre's injuries. Dre looks at him and says, "I thought you were just a maintenance man." Mr. Han says, "You think only with your eyes. So, you are easy to fool."[5]

That's the problem the Pastor's shaking his readers out of. They're thinking with their eyes. In the context of this book, what seems real to them is the old order of worship, the tabernacle, the priests, the sacrifices. We have already seen how the Pastor repeatedly tells them that those things are obsolete and ready to vanish away. They were just a shadow of the good to come (10:1). Setting their minds on those things is why they were easily fooled. It's the same with us. We think with our eyes. So if everything around me is good, then I'm good. If everything I see around me is messed up, then I'm messed up.

Do you know that it is possible for everything in our life to be going well and still be a mess? It's also possible for all hell to break loose around us and still be okay. What determines our ability to persevere is the object of our faith. What determines our ability not to become full of pride when things are going great and not to become completely crushed when life is hard is the object of our faith. What faith sees—or *perceives*—is Jesus.

Rather than describing biblical faith as a wish or a fantasy, the Pastor describes it in rock-solid terms. It's the assurance of what we hope for. Hebrews 11:1 is the last explicit mention of the word *hope* in the letter, and it comes in the context of defining faith. What we hope for is synonymous with "the things we don't see." Faith is assurance and conviction about the unseen. The things hoped for that we do not see have nothing to do with the American dream. The Pastor isn't saying, "Just believe hard enough and you'll get everything you ever wanted."

He talks about faith as conviction and assurance because he's gone to great lengths to highlight the heavenly realities. His readers needed the ability to see the heavenly reality that was the source of the earthly shadow. He defines this type of eyesight as faith. From the beginning of the letter, he's been talking about the reality that Jesus sat down at the right hand of the Majesty on high. He's there right now before the face of God the Father, advocating for his people. He makes perfect everyone who draws near to God through him. The Pastor has been telling them, "This is reality." And by faith we know it's certain. The commentator Philip Edgcumbe Hughes says, "Faith is a guarantee of the heavenly realities for which we hope; not only does it render them certain for us, but it envisages them as rightfully belonging to us; it is, in itself, an objective assurance of our definite enjoyment of them."[6]

The Pastor doesn't say, "By faith we *think* the universe was created by the word of God." No, by faith we *understand* that God spoke, and the universe was formed and framed at his command. By faith we understand that God said, "Let there be," and there was. Then he reminds his readers of Noah. If he thought only with his eyes, he never would've built the ark. But he was warned by God about things that were not yet seen, and he responded to the unseen reality with reverent fear, that is, with a godly devotion. Noah didn't care that he looked like a fool building an ark. By doing so, he saved his household, and by his faith he condemned the world, which didn't respond in faith to God's word. And he simultaneously became one in a long line of those who receive righteousness from God by faith.

What faith receives. What faith sees is Jesus. What faith receives is God's commendation. This faith is sanctioned by God. In other words, God himself puts his stamp of approval on people who have this faith. The Pastor says in 11:2, "The people of old, those who came before you Hebrews, by faith they received commendation" (author's translation). Received commendation from whom? The Pastor is talking about divine approval. The people of old received divine approval from God himself. That's what faith receives.

I live in Washington, DC, a city filled with professionals. In their various professions, they get all kinds of certifications and stamps of approval necessary for advancing in their careers. Whether you're a professional or not, we all want approval from someone for something. Even rebels want others to acknowledge the fact that they're rebellious. Everybody wants approval. And God, the creator of the universe, the only one who is eternal, unchanging, infinite, and all-powerful says that there is only one way for people to receive his stamp of approval—by faith. God commands us to believe, then he commends us for believing.

The Pastor starts his history lesson on faith by giving us two people of old who were commended by God. The word that's translated in Hebrews 11 as "commended" is the same verb that's normally translated as "testify" or "bear witness." The reason it's translated as "commend" in this chapter is because it's in the passive voice. It has the sense of someone being testified about, someone being spoken well of or approved. God is communicating that these are the people he speaks well of. These are folks he testifies about. That's wild if you think about it. How could it be that a holy and righteous God could have anything good to say about broken-down, sinful people? Well, God puts his stamp of approval on them and then he sanctions them, not for their perfection, but for their faith.

The Pastor says in 11:4, "By faith Abel offered a better sacrifice to God than Cain, through which he was approved as righteous. God bore witness by accepting his gifts. And because of this, although he died, he still speaks" (author's translation). He takes them back to Genesis 4 and the first case of murder in the Bible. Because of sin, sacrifice was now a necessity. Both brothers knew it, and both brought God an offering. But the Bible says that the Lord had regard for Abel and his offering, but he had no regard for Cain and his offering (Genesis 4:4-5). When Cain got angry, the Lord asked, "Why are you angry? If you do well will you not be accepted?" What was the Lord talking about? "Doing well" is living by faith.

At the end of Hebrews 10, the Pastor quoted from Habakkuk 2:3-4, where God says, "My righteous one shall live by faith." In his first example, he says that Abel was commended as righteous by faith. God testified that Abel was righteous by accepting his gifts. The difference was that Abel's heart was in the right place. What mattered was the integrity of his heart. It was directed toward God's word and his promise. In the chapter before the incident with Cain and Abel, God promises to send a Savior when he says to the serpent that he will put enmity between the serpent's offspring and Eve's offspring. Abel responded in faith to God's word and promise.

Even though he died, Hebrews 11:4 says he still speaks. How does he still speak? His faith still speaks to us. In the last words of chapter 10, the Pastor encourages his readers by saying we are of those who have faith and preserve their souls. Abel's faith speaks to the need for x-ray vision because even though he was murdered, he still lives! His testimony is that even though he paid the ultimate price for his faith, he still lives through God. He belongs to the number of those who have faith and keep their life, despite what it looks like. You endure by faith just like Abel endured by faith.

The Pastor's second example comes from Genesis 5. He says of Enoch, "By faith Enoch was taken so that he did not see death. And he was not found because God took him. For before the taking away he had been approved as pleasing to God" (11:5, author's translation). Cain and Abel are the first incident of murder. It can be argued that what we find in Enoch is the first miracle in Scripture. Enoch didn't see death. God took him directly from life on earth to life in God's presence. The Pastor says Enoch wasn't found because God took him, but he doesn't focus as much on the miracle as he does on Enoch's faith. By faith he was taken up. Before he was taken, he was commended. God testified that Enoch pleased him.

There was a point in Enoch's life when he began to trust God. Genesis 5:21 says that when Enoch had lived sixty-five years, he fathered Methuselah. Then verse 22 says that Enoch walked with God after the birth of Methuselah. God testifies again in Genesis 5:24 that Enoch walked with God. Walking with God is a fitting description of the Christian life, as it is similar to the idea of abiding with God that Jesus describes in John 15:4-5.

> Abide in me, and I in you. As the branch cannot bear fruit by itself, unless it abides in the vine, neither can you, unless you abide in me. I am the vine; you are the branches. Whoever abides in me and I in him, he it is that bears much fruit, for apart from me you can do nothing.

To say that Enoch pleased God is simply to say that he had faith. He walked with God. He abided in God. He understood where the source of his life came from. He saw behind the seen. He understood what the Pastor says in Hebrews 11:6, "Now without faith it is impossible to please him. Because the one who draws near to God must believe that he exists, and that he is a rewarder for those who seek him" (author's translation).

What faith seeks. The Pastor keeps talking in this letter about drawing near to God (4:16; 7:19, 25; 10:22). Here again in chapter 11, he says it for the sixth time. The individuals listed in this "hall of faith" drew near to God.

What faith sees is Jesus. What faith receives is divine approval from God. What faith seeks is to draw near to God. You want to draw near to God? You've got to believe that God exists. Literally, the Pastor says you've got to believe that God is. His readers would have been clear that he was pointing them back to their foundational confessional statement from Deuteronomy 6:4, "Hear, O Israel: The Lord our God, the Lord is one." In other words, anyone who comes to God needs to be straight on who God is. The one who would draw near to God by faith must do so seeking to know him as he is.

When the Pastor says that those who would draw near to God must believe that he exists and that he rewards those who seek him, he's talking about seeking grace through faith by repenting of our sins and turning to him. He's not talking about something new here. Drawing near to the throne of grace to receive mercy and find grace is the same thing as seeking God for his reward. The reward is not stuff. The reward is God himself, whose mercies are new every morning. The reward is God himself, who is gracious and merciful, full of steadfast love and faithfulness. The reward is God himself, who will never leave or forsake his people, who gives life to the dead, who renews the strength of his people so that they can endure. Faith seeks to draw near to God for grace because you cannot live by faith in the Lord Jesus Christ without looking and sounding foolish in the eyes of people who don't.

In the Winter 2017 edition of *Comment* magazine, physician Raymond Barfield wrote an article titled "Seeing the Beauty of Dappled Things" that includes the subtitle, "A poet taught a physician how to see again." The poet Dr. Barfield is talking about is nineteenth-century Jesuit priest Gerard Manley Hopkins, whom I mentioned in the last chapter. Dr. Barfield was experiencing burnout from his work. He said,

> I had lost my ability to see in the middle of institutional dysfunction and the never ending stream of urgent tasks demanding my attention. . . . So much of what we toil after, and trade our time for,

is bound to our attempts to stabilize a world that is teetering on change and dissolution.[7]

He describes the way out of this burnout for him as a different kind of seeing, "Over time, I discovered that one way past this crisis was to recover a kind of mindful wonder at the beauty that shows up in my work and life, even when the stories are hard or tragic."[8] The opening line in one of Hopkins's poems simply reads, "The world is charged with the grandeur of God."[9]

Are you able to see the grandeur of God in the mundane experiences of life in this world? To do so, Dr. Barfield rightly says, "the one seeing must be emptied of buzzing distraction and surrender to the seeing as a mode of love, love as agape and love as the fire of eros, a desire that consumes without destroying."[10] My friend Dr. Elissa Yukiko Weichbrodt uses the wonderful term "redeeming vision" to describe a hope-infused way of seeing that is also informed by the truth that God sees what does not yet exist and lovingly invites us into his vision. She writes,

> We find God's loving regard, his redeeming vision, throughout the Scriptures. . . . God sees sin—the cracks of the fall rupturing the wholeness that he made—but he locates it within the broader narrative of the restoration that he is bringing to bear. Someday, everything sad will become untrue.[11]

This is the motivation in drawing near to God by faith—the grace for eyes that see with lenses of love. It's true that communities are broken. It's true that people are broken. It's true that institutions are broken. It's true that we are broken. But it's truer that God is a redeemer and a healer. It's truer that he specializes in repairing what is broken. It's truer that God's promise cannot fail.

9

LIVE FOR THE CITY

I hope you hear inside my voice of sorrow
And that it motivates you to make a better tomorrow
This place is cruel, nowhere could be much colder
If we don't change, the world will soon be over
Living just enough, stop giving just enough for the city

STEVIE WONDER, "LIVING FOR THE CITY"

John Cotton, a prominent Puritan pastor, arrived in New England in 1633. Three years prior to that, while still in England, he had preached a famous farewell sermon to another group of Puritans who were making their departure across the Atlantic to New England. The title of the sermon was "God's Promise to His Plantation," and his text was 2 Samuel 7:10: "And I will appoint a place for my people Israel and will plant them, so that they may dwell in their own place and be disturbed no more. And violent men shall afflict them no more, as formerly." His emphasis in this sermon was that God was making room for his people in this new land, New England.

He said that when God "makes a Country though not altogether void of Inhabitants, yet void in that place where they reside. Where there is a vacant place, there is liberty for the sons of *Adam* or *Noah* to come and inhabit, though they neither buy it, nor ask their leaves."[1] God, in his sovereignty, places people in this or that country over all the earth, but in the text Cotton chose, a special appointment is in view as God speaks it by his own mouth. God's people take the land by promise. Therefore, the land of Canaan is called the land of promise. There is poor comfort sitting down in any place you cannot say is appointed for you by God.

In a very real sense, these Christians crossing the Atlantic to come to New England was metaphorically akin to Israel crossing the Jordan River to take possession of the Promised Land. It was to be a new and better country for them, where they would be able to escape the religious persecution they were enduring in England. But as we know, this "better city" wasn't so much better for everybody.

In 1973 Stevie Wonder put this trauma to music with his song "Living for the City," which tells the story of a young Black man trying to get out of the South to make a new life in New York City. He gets sent to prison and serves ten years for a crime he didn't commit.

> His hair is long, his feet are hard and gritty
> He spends his life walking the streets of New York City
> He's almost dead from breathing in air pollution
> He tried to vote but to him there's no solution
> Living just enough, just enough for the city [2]

What was viewed as the chance for a better city by the Puritans became the place of persecution for others. We can rightly criticize the Puritans for living as though New England was to be a place built by and for Christians. At the same time, we can identify with the longing for things to be better, whether we're Christians or not. That longing is a longing for God, and it's hard to endure with joy when that longing is so intense.

I love the way Saint Augustine put it when comparing the cities of this world and the city of God. He said, "One is the city of 'belongings' here in this world; the other is the City of 'longings' for God." [3] How do you live in the city of "belongings" in this world as citizens of the city of "longings" for God? This is what the Pastor begins to emphasize in Hebrews 11:8. In effect, he says, "God wants you to live like you're a citizen of heaven, not like you're a citizen of Palestine." This is the life of faith in

Jesus Christ. By faith in him, we are able to persevere through the ups and the downs, the ins and the outs of this life because we understand that we are citizens of the city of God.

The Pastor delivers this message by using Abraham as his example. Abraham gets more space in this chapter than any of the other "people of old." That's because Abraham was recognized as the father of the faithful. So he had credibility. If Abraham, by faith, lived like he was looking forward to a better city, a city with foundations, whose designer and builder was God, then what's your excuse? The Pastor's already told them in 2:16 that Jesus helps the offspring of Abraham. So, if you're one of those offspring, you ought to be living like it. You ought to be *living for the city*, that is, the city of God.

With Abraham as his example, the Pastor shows what living for the city of God looks like, as well as what it means to have your life now be formed by the reality of a heavenly homeland.

LIVING FOR THE CITY MEANS OBEDIENCE

The Pastor began his roll call of faith all the way back in Genesis with Abel and Enoch who were commended by God, who testified that they were faithful. Then he talked about Noah who, by faith, constructed an ark for the saving of his household and became heir of the righteousness that comes by faith. Now he says in 11:8, "By faith, when Abraham was called, he obediently went out to a place that he would later receive for an inheritance. And he went out with no idea where he was going" (author's translation). Faith is the assurance of the things we hope for. It is the conviction about the things we don't see.

Faith in the unseen undergirds this entire chapter. Abraham didn't know where he was going. He didn't know where this place he was to receive as an inheritance was going to be.

> And Abram took Sarai his wife, and Lot his brother's son, and all their possessions that they had gathered, and the people that they had acquired in Haran, and they set out to go to the land of Canaan.

> When they came to the land of Canaan, Abram passed through the
> land to the place at Shechem, to the oak of Moreh. At that time the
> Canaanites were in the land. Then the LORD appeared to Abram
> and said, "To your offspring I will give this land." So he built there
> an altar to the LORD, who had appeared to him. (Genesis 12:5-7)

God didn't tell Abraham the destination ahead of time. But when
Abraham heard God's call—when he heard the word of God—he responded with obedience. Living for the city means obeying the king of
the city.

That word *obedience* makes us nervous. It doesn't make us nervous
when it's in the context of other people obeying us. We definitely like that.
Parents all over the world would be smiling today if they knew that they
could get even one day of the year where their children were going to be
perfectly obedient. If they knew that today there would be no back talk,
no rolling of the eyes, no stomping, no grouchiness, no grumpiness because their child didn't want to do what they asked them to do . . . oh, the
joy that would fill a parent's heart if that were to happen! We're happy
when other folk obey us. What makes us nervous is when we've got to
obey someone else. That's because we're not in the driver's seat. But this
first point out of Hebrews 11:8 is that faith responds to the Word of God
with action. And the action is obedience.

Abraham was living in Ur of the Chaldeans, that is, Babylon. And he
didn't have a miserable life. His wife, Sarah, couldn't have children, but
he wasn't poor or struggling to make ends meet. Abraham didn't have any
reason to leave his homeland until the Lord God said, "Go from your
country and your kindred and your father's house to the land that I will
show you" (Genesis 12:1). And the Pastor reminds us that by faith, when
he was called to go, Abraham obeyed. God's word was enough for him to
leave his homeland without looking back. Both the text in Genesis and
our text here in Hebrews imply that Abraham's response was immediate.
The Lord said, "Leave here, and follow me to a place that I'm going to give

you as an inheritance. I'll let you know when you get there." Abraham's response was, "Let's go." The feet of faith are an obedient response to the word of God.

The other prominent examples of obedience in Hebrews 11 are Moses and his parents.

> By faith when Moses was born he was hidden for three months by his parents because they saw that the child was beautiful and they did not fear the king's edict. By faith when Moses grew up he refused to be known as the son of Pharaoh's daughter. Instead, he chose to be mistreated with the people of God rather than have a temporary enjoyment of sin. Because he considered the reproach of Christ was worth far more than the treasures of Egypt, he looked intently on the reward. By faith he left Egypt behind without fearing the king's wrath. For he endured as if he saw the invisible. By faith he had the Passover and the sprinkling of blood observed so that the one who was to destroy the firstborn would not harm them. By faith they crossed the Red Sea as through dry land. Which, when the Egyptians tried to do, they were swallowed up. (Hebrews 11:23-29, author's translation)

At the end of Genesis, things were going well for the Hebrews. Joseph had been the prime minister, second in command to Pharaoh. They had been given the land of Goshen in Egypt. Life was good. Just like life was good for Abraham when he was in Ur, life was good for the Hebrews in Egypt. They weren't thinking, *Let's get out of here, and go to the land God promised to give our fathers Abraham, Isaac, and Jacob.* They had abundance in Egypt. There was good fishing and farming. It was the most powerful nation in the ancient world. There was no need to go anywhere.

But God has a habit of upsetting our apple carts. He makes a good situation unbearable so that his people will wake up from the hypnotic effects of comfort and choose him over life's pleasures. So a new king rises over Egypt who doesn't know Joseph. He issues an edict and suddenly, their good life changes into a life of slavery. Then it gets worse. He commands his people, "Every boy you see that's born to the Hebrews, you take him and throw him into the Nile river and drown him, but let the girls live" (cf. Exodus 1:16). It's in the middle of that hellish existence that Moses is born. The Pastor says that because they saw that he was beautiful, they hid him for three months.

What parent doesn't think that their child is beautiful? We'd think something's wrong if a parent saw their baby and didn't think the child is beautiful. It doesn't matter if the child is theirs biologically or by way of adoption, a parent's heart is knit to their child. So, something more than their being overwhelmed by Moses' physical appearance is going on here. His parents make a present choice to defy an unjust law because of an inner conviction that the Lord has some divine purpose for this boy. By faith they said, "The government is wrong. We will not obey an unjust law." This is civic disobedience. They were risking their own lives by disobeying the law. But the Pastor says that they weren't afraid of the king's edict. God honored their choice, and Moses grew up in Pharaoh's house. But when he grew up, he had a choice to make. His faith was put to the test.

When we look at the tragedy of American slavery, we make a distinction between the house slave and the field slave. The house slave had it better than the slave who had to work out in the fields all day under the hot sun. If given a choice, you'd rather work in the house. Even though you're still a slave, there are more perks. But Moses' situation was better than that. He shared the same ethnicity as the slaves, but he lived like royalty. He wasn't living the life of a house slave in the palace. He was living the life of the master's son. His life as the adopted son of Pharaoh's daughter was nice.

The Pastor says that Moses made a choice when he grew up. He gave up the good life and refused to be called the son of Pharaoh's daughter, choosing rather to be mistreated with the people of God than to enjoy the fleeting pleasures of sin. Moses turned his back on his position of power and prestige. Did he have to do that? Joseph was in a position of power and prestige in Egypt, and he used that situation to help save God's people. Wouldn't you be tempted to try and make your case with God? When you examine the choice—back-breaking labor building cities for Pharaoh or trying to work for change within the government—wouldn't you at least be tempted to make the case? "You know God, I can serve you better within the government. My skills can be best utilized here on the inside, working for change here in the palace. I'll propose new policies that'll eventually provide better wages and working conditions for my people."

That might be a decent strategy in American governance, but God's purpose for Israel wasn't better working conditions. It was to bring them out of slavery. For Moses to try and hold onto his position of prestige and power would have meant him holding on to the temporary, decaying pleasures of sin. What was far more valuable to him was the reproach of Christ. Hebrews 11:26 is an incredible statement, "[Moses] considered the reproach of Christ of greater wealth than the treasures of Egypt, for he was looking to the reward." At this point, you may be wondering if the Pastor is trying to pull a fast one on us? Jesus wasn't born yet. How can Moses put a value on the reproach of Christ when he's never heard of Christ? And what is "the reproach of Christ" anyway?

The reproach of Christ is the insults and the persecutions, the sufferings that come from being associated with Jesus Christ. This will help us move toward what the Pastor is driving at. In Acts 9 when Saul, a man who persecuted and ravaged the church, was on his way to Damascus, a light from heaven flashed around him. He fell to the ground, blinded by the light, and heard a voice say to him, "Saul, Saul, why are you persecuting me?" Saul replied, "Who are you Lord?" and the voice responded, "I am Jesus, whom you are persecuting" (Acts 9:4-6).

When Saul was persecuting the people of God, he was persecuting their Messiah. Jesus is so united with his people that to persecute them is to persecute him. Moses decided he would rather be joined to the people of God and suffer with them because he believed God's promises to them. He made the present choice to endure suffering by faith because he focused his eyes on the heavenly, eternal reward. All the treasures of Egypt can't compare to what God has prepared for those who love him.

This is how the Pastor is weaving his message to encourage his readers to persevere. He's used the word *reproach* before in 10:32-33. Now he says when you were willing to be publicly exposed to reproach, you were doing only what the people of faith always choose to do. Moses did the same thing. God's people are always willing to choose insults and persecutions over abandoning the Savior. A feature of faith is that its present choices when faced with life's difficulties are based on the belief that spiritual riches are more valuable than material treasures. We should believe Jesus when he says in Matthew 5:11-12,

> Blessed are you when others revile you and persecute you and utter all kinds of evil against you falsely on my account. Rejoice and be glad, for your reward is great in heaven, for so they persecuted the prophets who were before you.

This is about identity. Moses didn't choose insults. He chose Christ and the insults came.

In 11:27, the Pastor makes a striking emphasis about the display of God's power to strengthen those who live by faith. He says that by faith Moses "left Egypt, not being afraid of the anger of the king, for he endured as seeing him who is invisible." This is a significant point when we think as Christians about social action. It's necessary to settle the identity question before determining the action question. In fact, it's our identity that ought to determine the nature of our actions. There are all kinds of cultural concerns that Christians and non-Christians alike are passionate about engaging in the civic arena. I live in Washington, DC, which means I get a front seat to regular protest marches. I participated in them as a much younger man and a non-Christian, and I've participated in protests as a Christian. What's the difference? Identity!

Moses protested the unjust system in Egypt as a young man by murdering an Egyptian overseer. As an old man, Moses confronted the injustice of Egypt to Pharoah's face without fear or violent rage. Secure in Christ, he was willing to bear reproach. Are you passionate about political issues, concerned about where our culture is in its approach to gender and sexuality, disturbed by ongoing racial injustice, or any number of other wearying aspects of our society? Your identity in Christ is what determines your action around all these things. In Christ, we are able to say with Paul, "We refuse to practice cunning or to tamper with God's word, but by the open statement of the truth we could commend ourselves to everyone's conscience in the sight of God" (2 Corinthians 4:2).

Moses left Egypt two times. The first time, he was afraid. The Pastor isn't talking here about that first time after Moses killed the Egyptian and had to run for his life. He's talking about the exodus and how Moses continually went before Pharaoh saying, "Thus says the Lord, let my people go." Again and again, he went in and stood before Pharaoh unafraid. What happened to the man who left Egypt the first time scared for his life? How could this man who ran away now stand before the most powerful man in the world? When he leads the people out of Egypt and they get to the Red Sea with Pharaoh's army in hot pursuit, the people say, "Why did you bring us out here to die? Is it because there were no graves in Egypt?" Moses says to them, "Fear not, stand firm and see the salvation of the Lord" (Exodus 14:11, 13).

How is it? The Pastor says that Moses endured as seeing him who is invisible. X-ray vision. Faith is the conviction about the things we don't see. By faith, Moses had his eyes fixed on the invisible, and he received power to persevere. The Pastor then points out how God demonstrated his power not only to strengthen, but to save those who live by faith. He recalls the first Passover when the Lord had the Israelites slaughter lambs and put the blood over the doorposts of their homes so that he would not strike down the firstborn of Israel. Then he reminds them of how God put his power on display when the people passed through the Red Sea on dry ground and the Egyptians were drowned when they tried to do the same thing.

If we're living for the city of God, the Word of God is sufficient reason for us to respond in obedience. This obedience is decisive action that demonstrates the reality of our faith, *especially* when there's a cost. If there's no obedient response to the Word of God, it's a clear demonstration that we don't have our sights set on heaven at all. The acts of obedience are related to the priorities of Christ's kingdom. This is a strong word, and I think that Dr. John Frame hits the nail on the head when he says,

> When we know that God has truly spoken and that he has announced his ultimate intentions, we have no right to question him. When he tells us something, we have no right to demand evidence over and above God's own word.[4]

Living for the city of God means obediently following the voice of God, when you don't know the cost, because you know that you can trust God.

LIVING FOR THE CITY MEANS TRUST

Living for the city means trusting the king of the city because you consider him faithful. Trusting the Lord's promise of a firm future, especially when things are rough, is what enables us to make the present choice to do good. It's that trust in the firm future that enables Moses and his parents to make the present choice to follow God and not fear Pharaoh. Abraham set out in faith because he had a firm grasp on God's promise of an inheritance. Trusting God's promise drove his actions.

Look at 11:9-12:

> By faith he went to live in the land of promise, as in a foreign land, living in tents with Isaac and Jacob, heirs with him of the same promise. For he was looking forward to the city that has foundations, whose designer and builder is God. By faith Sarah herself received power to conceive, even when she was past the age, since she considered him faithful who had promised. Therefore from one

man, and him as good as dead, were born descendants as many as the stars of heaven and as many as the innumerable grains of sand by the seashore.

Let me make an editor's note here. Verse 11 is a tricky verse to translate from the Greek text. The ESV takes Sarah, Abraham's wife, as the subject, but it's clear to me that Abraham is the subject of this entire paragraph—and that includes verse 11. So I prefer the 1984 NIV's translation, "By faith Abraham, even though he was past age—and Sarah herself was barren—was enabled to become a father because he considered him faithful who had made the promise."

I point that out because the Pastor is homing in on Abraham's unwavering trust of God that had him always looking forward to the fulfillment of God's promises. Even when he got to the land of promise and the Lord told him it is the land he is going to give him and his descendants as an inheritance, Abraham never owned any of it. In fact, Stephen, a man "full of faith and of the Holy Spirit" (Acts 6:5), gave a sermon in Acts 7 that got him stoned to death. He begins that sermon with his own history lesson, starting with Abraham. He says that God gave Abraham no inheritance in the land, not even a foot's length, but promised to give it to him as a possession and to his offspring after him, though he had no child (Acts 7:5).

Hebrews 11 reminds us that the entire time Abraham lived in the Promised Land, he lived as a foreigner. When Sarah died in Genesis 23 and it was time to bury her, Abraham said to the Hittites, "Give me property among you for a burying place, that I may bury my dead out of my sight" (v. 4). Living as a foreigner meant not having the rights and privileges of a landowner. He sojourned in the land of promise. He moved around in it. He didn't settle down and build a house. He lived in tents like he was just visiting for a while.

When we've decided that we're going to settle down, that we're going to make someplace our new home, we eventually buy a house. We establish roots in that city or town. But sometimes the pull from our original hometown makes us hesitant to think of somewhere else as our home. We still consider ourselves visitors to our new place. Abraham lived like a visitor in Canaan, but it wasn't because he was homesick for his father's land. When it was time to find a wife for Isaac, he sent his servant back to his homeland. The servant asked him in Genesis 24:5, "What if the woman isn't willing to follow me back to this land. Must I then take your son back to the land from which you came?" Abraham basically responded, "Under no circumstances are you to take my son back there. If the woman isn't willing to follow you, you're free from this oath of mine; just don't take my son back there."

It seems that Abraham had such a trust in God's promise to give his descendants the land of Canaan that he put out of his mind any thought of going back to live at home. No matter how difficult it was for him to live like a visitor, moving from place to place, never settled, there was no thought of going back to the security of his homeland. The Pastor's point in showing us how Abraham, by faith, endured through life in the Promised Land as a renter instead of an owner goes way beyond his trusting God for a piece of land. He says in 11:10 that Abraham was looking forward to the city that has foundations. The city whose designer and builder is God. What city is that? Is the Pastor saying that Abraham was looking forward to the day when his descendants would live in Jerusalem?

Isn't it obvious that "the city with foundations whose designer and builder is God" goes way beyond the land of milk and honey? Abraham considered the God who made the promise to be faithful, and he understood the inheritance that God promised to be nothing less than the city of God, the heavenly Jerusalem, the holy city it says in Revelation 21:2, "The new Jerusalem, coming down out of heaven from God, prepared as a bride adorned for her husband." A tent has no foundations, but the city God establishes does. Trusting God by faith that our citizenship is in heaven enables us to live like foreigners.

What does it look like to live as someone who's citizenship is in heaven? Paul says in Philippians 3:17-20,

> Brothers, join in imitating me, and keep your eyes on those who walk according to the example you have in us. For many, of whom I have often told you and now tell you even with tears, walk as enemies of the cross of Christ. Their end is destruction, their god is their belly, and they glory in their shame, with minds set on earthly things. But our citizenship is in heaven, and from it we await a Savior, the Lord Jesus Christ,

He counts everything as loss because of the surpassing worth of knowing Christ Jesus. Then he says to join in imitating him. If your citizenship is in heaven, then you don't live like your god is your belly, which doesn't just mean that you eat too much. To live like your god is your belly means to be consumed by material things. To live by faith in Jesus Christ means to be so sure about the future that you live for him today with a trust in his power.

The Pastor devotes more ink to Abraham in verses 17-19:

> By faith, when Abraham was tested, he offered up Isaac. Indeed, the one who received the promises began to offer up his only son, about whom it was spoken, "Through Isaac your offspring will be named." His thought was that God was able to raise *Isaac* even from the dead. From which, figuratively speaking, he did receive him back. (author's translation)

There are other examples from Abraham's life he could've chosen from to conclude his thoughts on Abraham's faith, but none of them would've had the impact that the binding of Isaac had. It's the place in Abraham's life where the Bible says that God put Abraham to the test.

God said to Abraham in Genesis 22:2, "Take your son, your only son Isaac, whom you love, and go to the land of Moriah, and offer him there as a burnt offering on one of the mountains of which I shall tell you." Isaac wasn't Abraham's only biological son. He had Ishmael also, but God called Isaac Abraham's "only son" because, as the Pastor reminds us in 11:18, he was the son of promise. He was the one through whom Abraham's offspring would be named. The promises would come through Isaac, and now, God was commanding Abraham to do the unthinkable and offer him up as a burnt offering on one of the mountains.

What does Abraham do? He gets up the next morning, saddles his donkey, takes Isaac, two of his servants, and the wood for the burnt offering and he goes to the place God told him to go. The journey takes three days. When they get there, Abraham and Isaac go up the mountain together. Abraham takes the fire and the knife, and Isaac carries the wood. Isaac says to his father, "Here's the fire and the wood, but where is the lamb for a burnt offering?" How do you answer that question? Abraham says, "God will provide for himself the lamb for a burnt offering."

The Pastor reminds his readers that Abraham bound his son Isaac and laid him on the altar of wood. He was in the act of offering up his only son, the son of promise, when as he took the knife to slaughter his son, the angel of the Lord stopped him and said, "Do not lay your hand on the boy or do anything to him, for now I know that you fear God, seeing you have not withheld your son, your only son, from me" (Genesis 22:12). But the Pastor leaves that part out. He doesn't focus on the Lord stopping Abraham. Instead, he focuses on the reason Abraham was willing to carry out this unthinkable act God commanded of him. He says that it was because Abraham "considered that God was able even to raise [Isaac] from the dead" (Hebrews 11:19). In other words, Abraham considered that God's promise to him to make him a great nation and to bless all the nations of the earth through his offspring was so firm that not even the death of Isaac was strong enough to stop it.

When he was taking Isaac up the mountain he said to his servants, "The boy and I are going over there to worship. We'll be back." When God called Abraham to leave his father's house and all he knew, Abraham obeyed and gave up his past. He was saying, "I trust you, Lord. I'm going to follow you. Everything I know, the source of my identity, my source of comfort, and all meaning for my life is here in Ur in my father's house. But I'm going to leave all of that behind because you have told me to do so." So, he'd already given up his past. But when the Lord commanded him to go to Mount Moriah and offer up Isaac, he was saying to Abraham, "I don't just want you to give your past to me. I want you to surrender your future to me also."

The Pastor is letting us know that faith is not just surrendering our past life of sin and rebellion to the Lord. It's also surrendering our future to him. Faith in God through Jesus Christ means total surrender—surrender of the past, surrender of the present, and surrender of the future—because we understand that our future is more secure in his control than it is in ours.

That's the same type of faith the Pastor is pointing out that was exhibited by Isaac and Jacob and Joseph in 11:20-22:

> By faith, concerning things that were to come later, Isaac blessed Jacob and Esau. By faith Jacob, when he was dying, blessed each of Joseph's sons. Then he bent in worship on the head of his staff. By faith Joseph, at the end of his life, had the exodus of the children of Israel in mind and gave instruction concerning his bones. (author's translation)

The example he gives for each one of these men is at the end of their lives. They did not receive the things promised, but because they understood that the future was firm in God's hands, they didn't die miserable, depressed, and despondent. They died full of faith, so much so that Isaac pronounced future blessings on Jacob and Esau. Jacob, in an act of worship, blessed Ephraim and Manasseh, Joseph's sons. Joseph died in Egypt saying, "The Lord's going to bring you all up out of here. When he does, make sure you take my bones with you and bury them in the Promised Land."

Are we living for the city in a way that demonstrates we are trusting our future to the Lord? Or do our actions communicate that we are only fine with giving God control when things are going well? Don't you realize that God is still in the testing business of seeing whether you've surrendered your future to him? He didn't stop with Abraham.

Peter, "Beloved, do not be surprised at the fiery trial when it comes upon you to test you, as though something strange were happening to you. . . . Therefore, let those who suffer according to God's will entrust their souls to a faithful Creator while doing good" (1 Peter 4:12, 19). Here's what we are repeatedly called to do: trust in God's power. A feature of faith is trusting in God's power to strengthen his people. Do we think that the power God has displayed in the path to strengthen his people in the past makes him unable to give us strength to endure today? No. Faith recognizes that we're weak, but he's strong. Faith recognizes that we can't, but he can and will. Faith is not paralyzed by fear. Faith perseveres by the power of God.

LIVING FOR THE CITY MEANS CLARITY

Abraham became wealthy but notice that the Pastor makes no mention of his material wealth at all—not because it's evil to be wealthy or righteous to be poor, but because living for the city of God means trusting in God and not in our stuff. Living for the city means obeying the Word of God because you trust God, and you trust him because you have clarity on where your real homeland is.

While focusing on Abraham, the Pastor zooms out for a moment in 11:13-16.

These all died in faith, not having received the things promised, but having seen them and greeted them from afar, and having acknowledged that they were strangers and exiles on the earth. For people who speak thus make it clear that they are seeking a homeland. If they had been thinking of that land from which they had gone out, they would have had opportunity to return. But as it is, they desire a better country, that is, a heavenly one. Therefore God is not ashamed to be called their God, for he has prepared for them a city.

Abraham, Sarah, Isaac, and Jacob were all still living by faith when they died because they had clarity of vision. They did not receive the things that were promised, but they were able to see and welcome the promises from afar. The promises of God were so clear and certain to them that even though they did not physically materialize in their lifetime, they could still see them clearly.

Cloudy vision often hinders us from living for the city of God, and difficulty can make things foggy. You see it again and again in Hebrews as the Pastor reminds his readers, "We're not of those who shrink back and are destroyed, but of those who have faith and preserve their souls" (Hebrews 10:39). They're dealing with opposition to their faith, and it's making things cloudy.

There are plenty of places in this world where Christians are dealing with direct opposition to their faith, which can either cloud or clarify what we're living for. The Pastor's heart desires for the suffering of his readers to serve as clarity. Those of us in the United States who perceive a growing hostility to Christianity within our culture must take care, however, to discern when it is directed at a rejection of the clear priorities of Christ and his kingdom and where it targets a false, syncretistic version of Christianity. The Pastor will exhort his readers in 12:14 to strive for peace with everyone and for the holiness without which no one will see the Lord (more on that in the next chapter).

There can be no doubt that God prioritizes our sanctification, that is, our growth in holiness (Hebrews 2:11). Holiness always includes righteousness and justice, which are the foundation of God's throne (Psalm 89:14). We should expect the church to struggle in its practical pursuit of righteousness and justice because sin remains, *and* we should expect to find those priorities resisted in our governments and institutions. The question is how do we respond? The response of faith is not to wage culture wars. The response of faith is to lead with love in a way that will often look like loss to the world.

This is how we avoid syncretistic religion that merges Christianity with the political ideology or national patriotism. As Kevin Smith, my friend, mentor, and former pastor used to say, "The kingdom of God isn't coming in on Air Force One." My point is not to offer an opinion on your choice of political party or politician, but rather to say that the drift into syncretism can be very subtle. And that kind of religion *should* be resisted by Christian and non-Christian alike. The church must live like citizens of a different kingdom.

I love the way this is emphasized in Hebrews 11:14, "For people who speak thus make it clear that they are seeking a homeland." People who confess that they are strangers and exiles on the earth are making it clear that they desire a homeland. The Pastor clarifies in 11:15 that the homeland Abraham and his family were thinking of wasn't Ur of the Chaldeans. If that's what they were thinking of, they could've gone back there when things got rough in Canaan. Instead, they desired a better country (11:16), specifically a heavenly homeland. The "better country" the people of faith desired wasn't another piece of land somewhere on earth free of problems for Christians. People of faith persevere because they're clear that this better country doesn't exist in the here and now. This clear desire for a heavenly homeland is what informs their life of faith here on earth.

Look with me at how the Pastor connects the faith of the people of old with the lives of the people to whom he's writing. Remember what he wrote in 10:32-36:

> But recall the former days when, after you were enlightened, you endured a hard struggle with sufferings, sometimes being publicly exposed to reproach and affliction, and sometimes being partners with those so treated. For you had compassion on those in prison, and you joyfully accepted the plundering of your property, since you knew that you yourselves had a better possession and an abiding one. Therefore do not throw away your confidence, which has a great reward. For you have need of endurance, so that when you have done the will of God you may receive what is promised.

To paraphrase, he's saying, "You know what it's like to live for a better city. You know what it's like to suffer the plundering of your property because you knew you had a better possession! When you lived like that you were just joining in the history of those who live by faith. Don't stop now! Persevere through to the end!" Can I tell you something? You can't live as a Christian without this same testimony. There will always be evidence in our lives of the Spirit of God enabling us to suffer some type of loss with joy because he has given us clarity that we have a better possession.

LIVING FOR THE CITY MEANS NO SHAME

Do we have clarity that heaven is our homeland? Not heaven as a dreamy place in the clouds like it was pictured in *Heaven Can Wait*, the film I referenced earlier, but heaven as the better city with better foundations, a city not subject to decay or destruction. Clarity is necessary here because every culture in every place throughout all time wants to set the conditions for the good life according to its own standards. You can't live life apart from faith in Jesus Christ and then assume that the better city we all long for will become your home.

The Bible is clear that to have heaven as your homeland requires faith in the Son of God, Jesus Christ. You can't live like the homeland you desire is the one you've got right now and then say, "I'm going to heaven." The Pastor says that people who desire the better homeland, the heavenly one, make a confession. They confess by faith in God and his promises that they are strangers and exiles right now, and there's evidence in their life to that effect. They're not just giving lip service.

For people like this, there's no shame in their game. Living for the city means no shame. A life of faith in Jesus Christ may certainly mean that other people put you to shame, but where it counts there's no shame at all. The Pastor says, "Therefore, because they desire a heavenly homeland, God is not ashamed to be called their God." Why? "He has prepared for them a city" (11:6).

God was not ashamed to be called the God of Abraham, Sarah, Isaac, and Jacob because he prepared for them a city with foundations. He designed it and he built it. And he's not ashamed to be your God either through faith in the Son of God:

> For it was fitting that he, for whom and by whom all things exist, in bringing many sons to glory, should make the founder of their salvation perfect through suffering. For he who sanctifies and those who are sanctified all have one source. That is why he is not ashamed to call them brothers. (Hebrews 2:10-11)

Almost like bookends, at the beginning of the letter and toward the end of the letter the Pastor emphasizes that God is not ashamed. God's lack of shame is seen in his willingness to send his Son to suffer for us. Now his lack of shame is seen in the fact that he's prepared a city for us.

FACING THE IMPOSSIBLE

In his history lesson on faith, the Pastor has moved from the early chapters of Genesis through the lives of Abraham, Isaac, Jacob, and Joseph and on to Moses and the exodus and the display of God's power to deliver his people as he parted the Red Sea for Israel to cross. But there's a big gap in this history lesson of faith between verses 29 and 30.

Verse 29 is the crossing of the Red Sea, "By faith the people crossed the Red Sea as on dry land, but the Egyptians, when they attempted to do the same, were drowned." Then he skips the rest of Exodus, Leviticus, Numbers, and Deuteronomy. He jumps all the way to the book of Joshua and the conquest of Joshua. "By faith the walls of Jericho fell down after they had been encircled for seven days" (Hebrews 11:30). The Pastor skips the whole wilderness generation. Why does he do that? Because he's already used them as a negative example in chapters 3 and 4. He's already said those are the jokers you don't want to be like. They're examples of those who refused to live by faith.

So he skips forty years, and beginning with the conquest that Joshua lead, he says,

> By faith the walls of Jericho fell after they were encircled for seven days. By faith Rahab the prostitute was not destroyed with the disobedient because she received the spies peacefully. And what more shall I say? For time would fail me if I gave a detailed account about Gideon, Barak, Sampson, Jephthah, David, and also Samuel and the prophets. (Hebrews 11:30-32, author's translation)

Everyone mentioned here faced impossible odds. Jericho was a city fortified by walls. Israel had no chance of conquering Jericho unless the walls were breached, but it was impossible for them to do. Rahab was a Gentile and a prostitute who lived in Jericho. How was she going to escape being killed when the city went up in flames? If she welcomed the Israelite spies, she put her own life in danger. Gideon went out to battle the Midianites with an army of thirty-two thousand men, but then God has him reduce the army to three hundred men. Nonetheless, Gideon's three hundred were successful. Barak defeated the Canaanites. Sampson, blinded and imprisoned, defeated the Philistines. David escaped Saul's sword to become the king of Israel. Samuel, the last of the judges and the first of the regular prophets, powerfully interceded for Israel at Mizpah and God broke the stronghold the Philistines had on Israel.

All these people succeeded in impossible situations by faith. The walls of Jericho fell. Rahab lived. Gideon, Barak, Sampson, Jephthah, David, and Samuel conquered. The Pastor describes their successes in 11:33-35 as conquering kingdoms, enforcing justice, obtaining promises, stopping lion's mouths, quenching fire, escaping the edge of the sword, being made strong in weakness, becoming mighty in war, and putting foreign armies to flight. It all took place by faith in the God who specializes in doing the impossible. Impossible success is possible by faith because, as Jesus says in Mark 10:27, "With man it is impossible, but not with God. For all things are possible with God."

When we talk about God's ability to do the impossible, we shouldn't get confused. God can give you desirable things like material possessions and health. Indeed, whatever desirable things we have we've been given them from God (1 Corinthians 4:7). But in the context of the Pastor's example, the impossible successes that God's people received by faith were not summed up in material possessions or individual desires.

Notice what they were doing. The point of commendation was their trust in the Lord's faithfulness to his promises. These promises were centered around God's commitment to save his people. It was a trust that God would deliver his people out of impossible situations. So the impossible success is with respect to the things of God. These successes *did* have a material and physical outcome. There was indeed benefit and blessing in the here and now. But they were not just physical victories—they were spiritual victories. God's purposes were fulfilled. He advanced his kingdom through these victories. They took place in the here and now, but they were successes that made heaven rejoice! That's the question. Are the victories we're seeking victories that will make heaven rejoice or simply make us happy?

There's another reason why these successes were impossible. It's not just because these folks faced impossible odds. Did you notice any character issues in the folks the Pastor mentions here? Every one of them faced impossible odds, and every one of them had questionable character issues. Israel conquered Jericho, but they were a stiff-necked people. Rahab was a prostitute. Gideon was scaredy-cat. He didn't want the call to save Israel. Jephthah was the son of a prostitute (Judges 11:1). Not only that, but he made a horrible vow and sacrificed his daughter (Judges 11:31). Sampson was ruled by his lust for women. No one's character was without blemish, not even David or Samuel. Couldn't the Pastor have chosen some better examples?

If we think that the Pastor is saying that God is cool with their poor choices, we're missing the point. He's already devoted a lot of ink to talking about sin in this letter. Here's the point. I can't put it any better than John Calvin did when he said,

> There was not one of them whose faith did not halt. . . . Thus in all
> the saints, something reprehensible is ever to be found; yet faith,
> though halting and imperfect, is still approved by God. There is,
> therefore, no reason why the faults we labour under should break
> us down, or dishearten us, provided we by faith go on in the race of
> our calling.[5]

If we were honest with ourselves, we would marvel at the fact that we
experience any success at all. The character flaws of the people mentioned
in these verses are not unique to them. We might look at them and shake
our head, but Calvin is right. In every saint there is always to be found
something reprehensible. The success seems impossible not just because
of their situation, but because of their character. When you look at their
character flaws, you say, "These people don't deserve to be successful."
They are unlikely candidates.

By including people with great faults and character flaws in the hall of
faith, the Pastor is showing us that God has always chosen what is foolish
in the world to shame the wise. He has always chosen what is weak in the
world to shame the strong (1 Corinthians 1:27-28). God never commends sin. What he does in people who live by faith in Jesus Christ is do
the impossible while he's changing you from the inside out.

In addition to pastoring the church we planted, I served as an associate
chaplain for a local jail ministry in our county. On one occasion, I spent
the better part of a day doing a ride along with a county police officer. It
was interesting talking to him about his job. There wasn't a lot of action,
and we had plenty of time to talk from early morning to mid-afternoon.
The last stop of the day was at the detention center. Because I was a
chaplain, I'd been at the detention center plenty of times. However, I'd
never been in the central booking facility where the officer had to go.

While I was waiting in central booking for the officer to finish his work,
some of the incarcerated women were cleaning the office I was sitting in.
One of them recognized me from the worship services we did for the

women every other month. She began to tell me a bit of the story of her life, and it's one I'd heard repeated by some of the other inmates over the years. She would have called herself a Christian before she was incarcerated there at the jail, but her faith didn't become something real and meaningful until she got there. At the detention center, she'd come to see that not only did she stand guilty before the judge, but without faith in Jesus Christ she stood guilty before God.

And her life was transformed in the jail. She has a boldness to her faith that enables her to encourage not only other inmates, but also her husband and her son when she speaks with them on the phone. And while she was waiting to get out and return home, she knew that it was God's divine design for her good that she ended up in jail. She knew that she would leave that place a different woman than she was when she entered. The truth that we don't like is that our faith is forged in adversity. It's the difficult situations that confront us with the question of whether our hope really is in the Lord or in something else. That sister found faith in the middle of the fire.

The fact that God can and does use ordinary messed-up people to do extraordinary things when they live by faith in Christ should get us excited. But if that excites us, what comes next frightens us. The same God who blesses his people with impossible success also strengthens his people to persevere through impossible suffering. The Pastor makes a transition in 11:35 from success to suffering. He stops naming names, but he probably had people in mind like the prophet Jeremiah, who was stoned to death according to tradition; or perhaps Zechariah, who was stoned to death in 2 Chronicles 24. He might have been thinking about Isaiah, who was sawn in two.

But there were clearly many more he had in mind because he writes in plural terms. He says in 11:35-38,

> But others were tortured as they rejected their release, so that they might obtain a better resurrection. While others received the

experience of mockings and scourgings in addition to chains and imprisonment. They were stoned. They were sawn in two. They died by murder with a sword. They went about in sheepskins, in goatskins. They were poor. They were oppressed. They were mistreated. They were people of whom the world was not worthy, as they wandered about on desert lands, hills, caves, and holes in the ground. (author's translation)

Some who lived by faith experienced success while others who lived by faith experienced suffering. All we really want to experience is success and victory, but the fact of the matter is that God gives some people the strength to *suffer* rather than to conquer. Some escaped the edge of the sword, became mighty in war, and put foreign armies to flight (11:34). Others were killed with the sword (11:37). The life of faith in Jesus Christ involves both impossible success and often impossible suffering, and we don't always get the choice of which one comes our way. We saw the character issues of the people described in 11:31-32. So it's not the case that if you do everything right as a Christian you are guaranteed success. The opposite is also true. It's not that if you're suffering as a Christian, it's because you're doing everything wrong.

The more important question is whether we are living by faith. Because God may send success or suffering our way and in either case, it's for his glory and our own good, as hard as it may seem. Part of his purposes, as we've already said, is to grow our sense of trust in him. If we endure impossible suffering and come out of it with our faith intact, it's only because God strengthened us. We see the contrast between success and suffering in 11:35, "Women received back their dead by resurrection. Some were tortured, refusing to accept release, so that they might rise again to a better life."

The film *Freedom Riders* is a documentary about the freedom rides of 1961 organized by the Congress of Racial Equality to challenge unjust segregation laws in the South. Both Blacks and whites, men and women who participated in the rides were brutalized and badly beaten by mobs of angry white segregationists. Some were mocked. Some were imprisoned. The movement eventually got the attention of President Kennedy, and he sent journalist and aide John Seigenthaler as a representative of his office to try to make sure there was no more violence. Seigenthaler was interviewed in the documentary and talked about what happened when one of the buses rolled into Montgomery, Alabama. The mob first destroyed the equipment of the reporters and then they attacked the riders.

Jim Zwerg, a white freedom rider, said that as he was being beaten he asked God to give him the strength to remain nonviolent and to forgive his attackers. Seigenthaler said that his heart was in his throat. As the mob was beating the riders, he described a skinny young man dancing in a boxing pose throwing punches at one of the Black women riders. As she turned, he could see the blood running from her nose and mouth. Seigenthaler grabbed her by the wrist to put her in his car, but she put her hands on the door and stopped him from saving her. She said to him, "Mister, I don't want you to get hurt. I'm nonviolent and I'm trained to take this. Please, don't get hurt. We'll be fine."

When you see the picture of Jim Zwerg leaning against a wall, face bruised, blood flowing from his nose and mouth onto his suit, you ask yourself, *How could he endure such suffering, and at the same time pray for his attackers?* When you hear the account of the woman who chose to be beaten rather than be saved, you wonder, *Why would anyone do that?*

There's a funny moment in documentary when another batch of riders get to Mississippi. The governor of the state decided that there would be no violence, but he planned to teach the riders a lesson by throwing them into the state penitentiary. As they were being put into the vehicle, one of the riders, Rev. C. T. Vivian, hadn't been arrested. He said they were about to close the door of the paddy wagon when he went up to the police captain, tapped him on the shoulder, and said, "I'm with them." He said the police chief turned his head away for a few seconds because he was smiling. He'd never seen anybody volunteer to be arrested. He had to compose himself and then put his stern face back on.

What was wrong with these people? Had they lost their minds? In the eyes of many, yes. To endure impossible suffering by faith is an intolerable thought, but these were people who refused to accept release and were willing even to suffer death because they understood that they had a better resurrection in Christ that physical death could never take away. With this kind of faith in the background, the Pastor is going to say in 12:4, "In your struggle against sin you have not yet resisted to the point of shedding your blood." Don't look at these people of faith who were destitute and poor, who were oppressed and mistreated and think that something was wrong with them. The life of faith in Jesus Christ involves rejecting worldliness. It involves rejecting sin and ungodliness, both in individuals and institutions. When you reject the world, the world often wants to eject you.

The God who gives impossible success is the same God who enables impossible suffering. In victory we are reminded of being united to Jesus Christ in his victory over the world. In suffering we are reminded of our union with Jesus Christ in his sufferings that led to his resurrection. That's the point. As the Pastor wraps up the chapter, he concludes by letting us know that God's plan is impossibly better than anything we could come up with. Whether you are currently enjoying success or enduring suffering, if your faith is in Jesus Christ, it is impossible to be in any better situation spiritually speaking. Why? Because through Jesus Christ, God makes people perfect.

Look at how he ends the chapter, "And these all, although they were commended on account of their faith, did not receive the promise because God provided something better on our behalf so that apart from us they would not be made perfect" (Hebrews 11:39-40, author's translation). When he says "these all," he's not just referring to the people in 11:30-40. He's talking about everyone in the whole chapter, all the "people of old"—Abel, Enoch, Noah, Abraham, Moses, and so on. None of them received what was promised. They didn't obtain the eternal inheritance. Jesus hadn't come yet, so Abraham died still looking forward to the city that has foundations, whose designer and builder is God. They were still looking for the better country, the heavenly one. Why did God allow them to die without receiving the promise? Because, the Pastor says, "God provided something better on our behalf so that apart from us they would not be made perfect" (11:40).

God, in his grace, reserved the perfection that he planned for his people in Jesus Christ until we could share it with them. God didn't have one plan for Old Testament believers and another plan for us. It's the same plan. They looked forward to his coming, but it's better for us because we can look back and know that Jesus did come. There's no mystery. We don't have to wonder about whether God is going to save. They had faith even though they only had a tiny spark of light about God's Messiah. For us, all excuses are taken away. Jesus shines brightly as the Savior of the world. Any excuse we can come up with not to put our faith in Jesus Christ is taken away. We were already told in 10:14 that by the single offering of himself on the cross, Jesus has perfected for all time those who are being sanctified. It doesn't get any better than that.

The life of faith in Christ is impossibly better because you can't improve on perfection. But what does that mean? We've seen in the examples from this chapter that it doesn't mean that we're going to get everything right. To be made perfect means to share in Christ's perfection. He was and is perfect. To belong to him means to have a share in his perfection. So, in Christ it's impossible to be in a better spiritual condition. That's why the Pastor can say that for the Christian, your heart is sprinkled clean from an evil conscience (10:22). That's why we're told again and again in this letter to draw near to God. That's why he can say in Christ we have a better hope (7:19). In Christ we have a better covenant (7:22). In Christ we have better promises (8:6). He's a better sacrifice (9:23). In him we have a better possession (10:34), a better city (11:16), a better life (11:30).

When you really grasp the fact that in Jesus God's plan is better, God makes us perfectly able to meet with impossible success and not become arrogant, and he makes us perfectly able to endure impossible suffering and not be crushed.

10

RUN THROUGH EXHAUSTION

Fatigue has both a physiological and psychological component. When you deplete your glycogen stores, for example, you become physiologically tired. . . . The message goes to your brain. . . . "Why am I doing this?" Such thoughts are familiar to most of us during moments of extreme exhaustion.

JERRY LYNCH AND WARREN A. SCOTT,
RUNNING WITHIN

A common implement in CrossFit workouts is the Concept2 rower. While I despise running, I enjoy rowing. In the 2018 CrossFit Games, one of the early surprise tests was a marathon, but on the rower! A marathon row is 42,195 meters, or 26.2 miles. Following the games a few members of my gym decided to train for a marathon row. Prior to this adventure, I'd never rowed more than 5,000 meters in one session. We set the date for our marathon as December 1, 2018, and put a plan in place from September through November. It began with multiple 10-kilometer rows per week followed by a 15-kilometer row. The next increase was a half-marathon, 21.1-kilometer rows. Eventually, a week out from the marathon, the row distance was 30 kilometers. When I completed that last long-distance row before the marathon date, I thought to myself, *That really hurt. How am I going to make it 42.2 kilometers?*

I experienced thoughts similar to what authors Jerry Lynch and Walter Scott address in their book *Running Within*.

Fatigue has both a physiological and psychological component. When you deplete your glycogen stores, for example, you become physiologically tired. . . . The message goes to your brain. . . . "Why am I doing this?" Such thoughts are familiar to most of us during moments of extreme exhaustion.[1]

To complete a marathon means learning to run (or row, in my case) through the exhaustion. Fatigue and weariness set in. It's inevitable. This is one reason why many people who start a marathon don't actually finish.

The marathon analogy is perfect for what embodied hope looks like. As the Pastor begins to wrap up his word of exhortation, he tells his readers they have need of endurance. He's pointing out that the life of faith in Jesus Christ is like running a race that God has marked out for you, and you need to endure. When fatigue sets in, the danger of dropping out is always close at hand. Embrace the reality that there's no way to run the race without facing fatigue or exhaustion. So if you're going to finish, you must have a compelling reason to run along with the strength to press through the fatigue. God both calls and empowers his people to run through the exhaustion. The compelling reason to run through the exhaustion is Jesus, who is both our example of faithful endurance and the source for the strength we need to endure.

One cause for the exhaustion Christians are experiencing today is the division in society and the church primarily around issues of race and justice. In 2021, Barna, in partnership with the Racial Justice and Unity Center, produced the report "Beyond Diversity: What the Future of Racial Justice Will Require of U.S. Churches." They wanted a "multidisciplinary, multifaceted methodology to investigate racial dynamics in the U.S. and in the Church."[2] The book *Divided by Faith: Evangelical Religion and the Problem of Race in America* brought to light the stark divide between white Christians and Black Christians on matters of racism and justice.

Following its release, interest in multiethnic churches exploded. Many saw them as the solution to our racial divides.

Beyond Diversity followed up on that work twenty years later with research conducted in 2019 and 2020. Dr. Michael O. Emerson writes, "In some ways, on some measures, things are even worse than they were 20 years ago. How could that be?"[3] Their research demonstrated that in the year following the racial reckoning of 2020, "the proportion of practicing Christians who are unmotivated to address racial injustice increased by thirteen percentage points."[4] When asked "Do you think our country has a race problem?" 38 percent of white practicing Christians responded "definitely," while 78 percent of Black practicing Christians gave the same response—a 40 percent gap. Fifty-six percent of Hispanic participants said "definitely," and Asian respondents matched whites at 38 percent. Of course we're exhausted! The question is how do we run through the exhaustion together?

Let me put on my personal trainer hat and offer some coaching points.

STAY WITH THE CROWD

"For this very reason, since we have so great a cloud of witnesses surrounding us, let us lay down every weight and the sin which controls us so tightly. Through endurance let us run the race set before us" (Hebrews 12:1, author's translation). The great cloud of witnesses the Pastor refers to in this verse are the members of the hall of faith in chapter 11, of whom he says the world was not worthy. You see, the race the Pastor is describing is neither a sprint nor a relay race where we each run our leg of the race and pass the baton on to someone else. It's a marathon—a strange marathon. We don't compete as individuals. We're not trying to win the race and beat everybody else. It's a marathon that we run with a bunch of other folks who are in the race with us, and the goal is not to break away from the pack and cross the finish line. The goal is that we all run together and cross the finish line together. We have emphasized at several points in this book the imperative for community if we are going to hold tightly to the hope set before us in Christ. And here we are again.

The apostle Paul likes to use the race metaphor in his letters. At the end of his life, he wrote, "I have fought the good fight, I have finished the race, I have kept the faith" (2 Timothy 4:7). Elsewhere, he says,

> Every athlete exercises self-control in all things. They do it to receive a perishable wreath, but we an imperishable. So I do not run aimlessly; I do not box as one beating the air. But I discipline my body and keep it under control, lest after preaching to others I myself should be disqualified. (1 Corinthians 9:25-27)

I refer to these texts because the life of faith in Jesus Christ is both individual and corporate. So there *is* a sense in which I'm running the race as an individual—but that's not the Pastor's primary emphasis. Every reference is to "we" and "us." Since *we* are surrounded by so great a cloud of witnesses. Let *us* lay aside. Let *us* run the race. The only time he speaks in the singular is when he refers to Jesus. His emphasis on the life of faith is corporate. It's life as the people of God running the race together.

He wants to see everybody cross the finish line, and it's been that way throughout the letter. He had said as much to them in chapters 3 and 4.

> But exhort one another every day, as long as it is called "today," that none of you may be hardened by the deceitfulness of sin. For we have come to share in Christ, if indeed we hold our original confidence firm to the end. . . . Therefore, while the promise of entering his rest still stands, let us fear lest any of you should seem to have failed to reach it. (3:13-14; 4:1)

The race we run in the church, we run together. We stay with the crowd. This can feel like empty words when the church is so polarized and seemingly unable to dialogue meaningfully and lovingly around the hard topics of our day. Even more, where there is open hostility expressed by Christians toward one another online. But that's precisely the point! The need for an embodied hope that keeps pressing to run together is most necessary when there is conflict. And when I read the first part of Hebrews 12:1, I get the image of a group of people running a marathon at around mile number seventeen. They've already run a long way, but they've still got a long way to go, and there's a large crowd on the sidelines who has already run the race and are cheering them on, helping them push past the exhaustion. If you've ever been a part of a competition and there's a large crowd cheering for you, you're able to keep going.

The Pastor says we are surrounded by a great cloud of witnesses. You're not the only one running the race. There is a rich history of faithful people who've run through the exhaustion and they're surrounding us. As the people of God live out their faith together, enduring through the difficulties and fatigue together, the cloud of witnesses should be a source of great encouragement because they're not just people who want to see us finish—they are people who have already run the race of faith all the way to the end. And they ran the race with less information than we have. They were looking forward to the promise of Jesus' coming. We look back at his coming. How do you run through exhaustion in the Christian life? It's not by a rugged individualism. Stay with the crowd that's surrounded by the cloud.

The question for the Christian is never simply, How am I doing at running the race? The question always includes, How are those around me doing running the race? Where are those around me starting to fade and fall off and lag behind? That's part of the reason why the race gets exhausting, and why we need supernatural strength to press on. It's because God calls his people to bear one another's burdens. He calls his people to carry those who are weak.

DROP THE WEIGHT

The race gets especially challenging when you're compelled by the gospel of Jesus Christ to see the local church look like its community in all of its diversity—Black, white, Asian, Latino, citizen, immigrant, rich, poor, young, old. Pursuing unity in diversity under the banner of Jesus Christ often results in increased cultural discomfort.

So, this vision, this pursuit of faithfulness to Christ by pursuing unity for the sake of the gospel is like running a weird sort of marathon. You run it together with a group of other folks who are running the same race. That's one way of talking about what the church is. By God's grace, he would have us run through the exhaustion by running together.

The second point is where it gets kind of sketchy. How do you run through the exhaustion? Well, you've got to drop the weight. The Pastor says, "Since we have so great a cloud of witnesses surrounding us, let us lay down every weight and the sin which controls us so tightly."

Recently, I purchased a weight vest to add more load to some of my training. If I have the time, I will walk a few miles in my weight vest after my workout. At the beginning of the walk, the additional weight doesn't feel too bad, but by the time I'm getting close to the end of the walk, all I want to do is take the weight vest off and drop it on the street. The walk would be so much better in the moment if I didn't have that vest weighing me down.

The Pastor's saying we can't run the race God has marked out for us if we're not willing to deal with the problem of our sin. When he says, "Let us lay aside every weight and sin which clings so closely," the verb translated as "lay aside" means to "lay down" or to "put away." It's used only nine times in the New Testament.[5] Seven of those times appear in the context of laying aside or putting away sin. Here are three examples.

- "The night is far gone; the day is at hand. So then let us *cast off* the works of darkness and put on the armor of light" (Romans 13:12).

- "But now you must *put them* all *away*: anger, wrath, malice, slander, and obscene talk from your mouth" (Colossians 3:8).

- "Therefore *put away* all filthiness and rampant wickedness and receive with meekness the implanted word, which is able to save your souls" (James 1:21).

It's hard to deal with sin. What about the cliques, the spoken and unspoken walls we allow to remain in the church, where we decide we can only do life according to our affinity groups? It's much easier to ignore sin, brushing it aside rather than engaging it. It's much easier to try to ignore it instead of confessing it.

But there's only one chapter in this whole letter where we don't find the word *sin*. The Pastor has been careful to show us how Jesus, by his sacrificial death on the cross, dealt with the problem of sin. But he's also been careful to show us that Jesus intercedes for his people before the face of God the Father, and that he helps his people overcome temptations. In chapter 2, he wrote, "Surely it is not angels that he helps, but he helps the offspring of Abraham. . . . Because he himself has suffered when tempted, he is able to help those who are being tempted" (vv. 16, 18). Do we really want to lay aside those things that are hindering our ability to run well, that sin of disunity that seems to control us so tightly? In the choices and the decisions we make as individual believers and churches every day, do we ask the question, Is this a help or a hindrance to God's call for us to be eager to maintain the unity of the Spirit in the bond of peace?

We've got weight that we need to drop if we're going to pursue this unity. The reason this gets sketchy is because we might nod our heads in agreement, but when the rubber meets the road our actions can give a different answer. Because this is hard. The Pastor didn't say, "Let us lay aside every weight and sin that bugs you every now and then." He said, "that clings so closely." He's not talking about the stuff we don't have a problem with. He's walking right up the street of the things that mess us up. If it were easy, he wouldn't have told us that Jesus helps his people. If it were easy, we could do it ourselves.

KEEP OUR HEADS UP

How do we run through exhaustion? We've got to stay with the crowd. We've got to drop the weight. And we've got to keep our head up. I don't mean any of this in the sense of a motivational speech a coach gives to a team when they're down in the dumps. I mean it in the sense of Psalm 121, where the psalmist says, "I lift up my eyes to the hills. From where does my help come? My help comes from the Lord, who made heaven and earth" (vv. 1-2). The Pastor says essentially the same thing in Hebrews 12:2. How do we run through the exhaustion? Look "to Jesus, the founder and perfecter of our faith, who for the joy that was set before him endured the cross, despising the shame, and is seated at the right hand of the throne of God."

Jesus is the founder of all true faith in God. That is, he is the pioneer of faith. The Pastor used this word previously in 2:10 when he said that it was fitting that God, "for whom and by whom all things exist, in bringing many sons and daughters to glory, should make the *founder* of their salvation perfect through suffering" (emphasis mine). There is no better example of faith for us to see or follow than the life of Jesus Christ. From beginning to end his life was one of perfect obedience. "Although he was a son, he learned obedience through what he suffered. And being made perfect, he became the source of eternal salvation to all who obey him" (5:8-9).

Recall what the Pastor said in 11:25-26 as he talked about Moses. Moses chose to be mistreated with the people of God rather than enjoy the fleeting pleasures of sin. Why? Because he considered the reproach of Christ greater wealth than the treasures of Egypt. In every age faith keeps its head up, focused on the Savior Jesus Christ. Keeping our head up and looking to Jesus is not simply about focusing on Jesus as our example. He's our example, yes, but the Pastor doesn't call us to look *at* Jesus. He says let us look *to* Jesus. Look to Jesus for help. Look to Jesus for strength. Look to Jesus for hope. Look to him in the sense of relying on him. Because he's not just the founder of faith. He's the perfecter of faith. A perfecter is someone who brings something to a successful conclusion. As the perfecter of our faith, Jesus brings us through to the end.

This verse is the fifth time in the letter where the Pastor tells us that Jesus has taken his seat in the position of power and authority at the right hand of God. Why so many times? Isn't it enough for him to have said it once and left it at that? He repeats himself so much because his readers are having trouble running the race. They're having trouble enduring through the point of exhaustion. It seems the powers of this world causing this trouble, both the people who are against them and their own sin, are stronger than the Savior they have trusted in.

So he reminds them and us repeatedly that Jesus is right now seated at the right hand of the Majesty on high. Jesus finished the work that the Father gave him to do. He endured hostility from sinners. He endured the cross, despising the shame. Throughout his entire life, as he endured the hostility, as he endured the suffering, as he endured the cross, what was set before him was *joy*. The road to the joy ahead of him was through the cross. That joy was an ever-present focus. His joy is not just being in the position of authority with the Father. The joy set before him was also to bring many sons and daughters to glory. We are included in Jesus's joy. The Pastor is saying, "Keep your head up." Look to Jesus. The things that cause us to grow weary and fainthearted are not stronger than Jesus.

Here's how I translate Hebrews 12:3, "For consider him who has endured against himself such hostility by sinners, so that you might not give out after your souls become tired." Some of us have exhausted souls. We feel as though our soul's strength has been emptied out. Do you understand that God is not surprised by that? Do you understand that you're not in some unusual place in the life of following Jesus? Do you understand that this exhaustion comes with the territory? The point of the passage is not that faithfulness to Jesus means that we won't get exhausted. It is that faithfulness to Jesus means that you *will* become exhausted. So sit in the fatigue and hear God saying, "I want you all to keep running *through* the exhaustion!" How? Keep your head up! We endure through the exhaustion by setting our focus on Jesus, the one who endured such hostility against himself from sinners.

In practice this means strengthening what is weak and straightening what is crooked, all with a sense of deep gratitude. If we're going to endure through this race, we've got to strengthen our drooping hands and our weak knees. That's the language the Pastor uses in 12:12. I know the ESV says, "Lift your drooping hands and strengthen your weak knees," but there's only one verb in the verse and it means to straighten up or strengthen. He applies it to two body parts—our hands and our knees. These body parts, he says, are weakened. Picture someone trying to run a race with their hands drooping down at their side and knees that are feeble and weak. How far are they going to get? If you're going to run the race well, you've got to strengthen what's weak.

Hebrews 12:12 starts with a "therefore." *Therefore*—because the Lord's discipline later produces the fruitful peace of righteousness (Hebrews 12:11)—God calls his people to strengthen the weak. In other words, the response to the Lord's corrective, loving discipline is not to be disheartened. Sin has caused his readers to be in danger. There are parts of the body that are lame, crippled, and at risk of falling off. These body parts are people in the community who are in danger because of sin. And the church does not discard people on the side of the road like dead weight because they struggle with sin.

Even though he's giving an athletic metaphor in 12:12, he's quoting Isaiah 35:3. The section he chooses to quote from in Isaiah appears at the end of a series of six laments in Isaiah 29–33 after which God begins to speak of the salvation that's going to come for those who persevere.

> The wilderness and the dry land shall be glad;
> the desert shall rejoice and blossom like the crocus;
> it shall blossom abundantly
> and rejoice with joy and singing.
> The glory of Lebanon shall be given to it,
> the majesty of Carmel and Sharon.
> They shall see the glory of the LORD,
> the majesty of our God.

Strengthen the weak hands,
    and make firm the feeble knees.
Say to those who have an anxious heart,
    "Be strong; fear not!
Behold, your God
    will come with vengeance,
with the recompense of God.
    He will come and save you." (Isaiah 35:1-4)

The Pastor concludes from this passage that the assurance of God's intervention provides the grounds to abandon anxiety and fear and to persevere in the race. The people of Isaiah's day had forsaken the Lord. They had turned to Egypt for help and protection instead of turning to the Lord.

Certain people among the readers of Hebrews were in danger of the same sin, abandoning the Lord and seeking other means because life wasn't as they wanted it. The reference to Isaiah 35:3 reminds them of the fact that they were not the first to experience weariness and fatigue in following the Lord. Christian maturity only happens in community. Sickness is sure to follow those who are not part of a healthy Christian community. The church is as much a hospital, a wellness center for sinners, as it is anything else.

The Pastor doesn't only say to strengthen what's weak, but he adds a nuance to it in 12:13 saying, "Straighten out what's crooked." Make straight paths for your feet. Here he's pulling from Proverbs 4:25-27.

Let your eyes look directly forward,
    and your gaze be straight before you.
Ponder the path of your feet;
    then all your ways will be sure.
Do not swerve to the right or to the left;
    turn your foot away from evil.

Make straight paths for your feet. Don't swerve to the right or to the left. Turn your foot away from evil "so that what is lame may not be put out of joint but rather be healed" (12:13). Again, it's people who are "lame" or "crippled" here, and the call is that we don't want anyone to be amputated from the body. The community of faith is a hospital. What we want is for the lame to be healed.

Thus, as we seek to persevere by faith in Christian community in our current culture of contempt, we must answer a key question: Do we want to see the Lord bring healing to what is lame and out of joint? In some ways, every Christian is lame or crippled. For strengthening, straightening, and healing to take place, the church has to be a safe place to deal with sin—full stop.

Several years ago, a friend of mine served in a ministry for formerly incarcerated men who'd been in prison for any length of time and were now out on parole. The ministry's focus was helping these men change. He told me about one guy who was embarrassed and ashamed his first time there because he had to wear an electronic ankle monitor as a condition of his parole. My friend told him, "You think you're the only one? Man, look around. We all have one of those." Practically everybody in the group had an electronic monitor.

It's interesting that my friend didn't tell the man, "They've all got one of those, you're just like them." He said, "*We* all have one," even though he himself had never been incarcerated. He identified himself with the group because he has a right view of sin. The way he addressed the guy's embarrassment said, "I don't stand above you. Your sin might be more obvious than mine, but we're in the same boat. So, this is a safe place to deal with your sin."

That's what the church is and ought to be. When the Pastor says that we don't want the lame body parts to be amputated but to be healed, the implication is that within the body of Christ, within the church, sinners have a safe place to deal with sin. The particular challenge today is not simply the divisions among Christians over political ideology, racism, justice, gender, and sexuality. The challenge is in the sinful way that we engage those divisions. If there is to be an embodiment of the hope we've been discussing throughout this book, *that* sinfulness must be addressed. The church is called to be a safe place for sinners to deal with sin.

FIXED ON THE FUTURE WITH GRATITUDE

The church becomes a safe place for sinners when we have our eyes firmly fixed on the future and our hearts resonate with the gratitude described in Hebrews 12:28. Exhausted souls burdened with sin, division, and fading hope need to remember these words:

> But you have come to Mount Zion and to the city of the living God, the heavenly Jerusalem, and to innumerable angels in festal gathering, and to the assembly of the firstborn who are enrolled in heaven, and to God, the judge of all, and to the spirits of the righteous made perfect, and to Jesus, the mediator of a new covenant, and to the sprinkled blood that speaks a better word than the blood of Abel. (Hebrews 12:22-24)

This is describing a present faith that is firmly fixed on the future. It doesn't mean that we live in denial of the problems and issues confronting us now. It means that we understand those things to be temporary. One day, they will be removed and done away with.

The Pastor begins to conclude his exhortation borrowing from the prophet Haggai who declared, "For thus says the Lord of hosts: Yet once more, in a little while, I will shake the heavens and the earth and the sea and the dry land" (Haggai 2:6). He tells his readers,

> At that time his voice shook the earth, but now he has promised, "Yet once more I will shake not only the earth but also the heavens." This phrase, "Yet once more," indicates the removal of things that are shaken—that is, things that have been made—in order that the things that cannot be shaken may remain. (Hebrews 12:26-27)

When God said, "Yet once more," he was making it clear that he's going to shake up the entire creation. You've got to live now with your faith fixed on this future hope because God is not content to let his creation continue forever dominated by sin and depravity. When God created the world, he pronounced a benediction. He proclaimed a blessing. He looked at all that he had made and saw that it was very good.

Why do we press into this broken world and church in hope with the priorities of Jesus Christ and his kingdom? Why do we strive to represent the king and the ways of his kingdom? Why do we apply his Word to bring healing and hope in a messed-up world? Is it because we think the road is supposed to be smooth and easy? Is it because we think we're not going to face resistance and conflict? No. It's because our eyes are firmly fixed on the future, and we know that our king is not content to let his creation continue forever dominated by sin and depravity. We know that the earth will be filled with the knowledge of the glory of the Lord as the waters cover the sea (Habakkuk 2:14).

We are reminded here that the current state of the world is not its final chapter. There is going to be a final doing away with the mess. God is going to remove the things that are shaken in order that the things that cannot be shaken may remain. The things that remain are those connected to the redemption that Jesus Christ brings.

God's grace is what enables us to live with that perspective. It's his grace that moves us to gratitude for a life of worship in his presence. The things that cannot be shaken will remain. "Therefore let us be grateful for receiving a kingdom that cannot be shaken, and thus let us offer to God acceptable worship, with reverence and awe, for our God is a consuming fire" (Hebrews 12:28-29). Here's the idea. Christians are those who are receiving an unshakable kingdom by grace. So, let's hold on to that grace because we're dependent on it.

Having a faith that is fixed on the assurance of God's future promise makes a difference in the here and now because people who have that faith are receiving the unshakable kingdom of God. My favorite definition for the kingdom of God comes from the pastor and theologian Geerhardus Vos: "To [Jesus] the kingdom exists there, where not merely

God is supreme, for that is true at all times and under all circumstances, but where God supernaturally carries through his supremacy against all opposing powers and brings man to the willing recognition of the same."[6] This is the kingdom Christians are receiving. The supernatural work of God carrying through his supremacy against the forces that oppose it!

Notice this. The writer doesn't say that since we are *building* the kingdom of God, let us hold on to grace or be grateful. We can be tempted to think that we're out there working for the Lord, helping him build his kingdom. The Pastor says, "Y'all ain't building nothing." God is the one who is building his kingdom. We get to participate as debtors to grace because we get the blessing of receiving the kingdom now. That's why it's an unshakable kingdom. It's not dependent on us!

LIGHTING UP THE DARKNESS

Here is the conclusion of the matter. Hope is not a hustle because the kingdom we have received is one that will never be destroyed. At the beginning of this book, I said that living in a broken and imperfect world means that threats to our deepest longings for peace will be the norm. The storms will continue to rage. We've learned that our hope is a sure and steadfast anchor of the soul in the middle of life's wearying storms.

I have written this book to invite us into an embodied hope that resists the urge to reduce faithfulness to Christ to waging culture wars effectively. You and I are invited by God into a hope that sees the life we live now with redeeming vision. This kind of hopefulness moves in the world by another way of being. The climate of our age is secularity. The weather patterns blow us to the poles of red or blue politics, affirming or homophobic, racist or antiracist, pro-choice or pro-life,[7] spiritual or religious. What we learn is that these poles are false choices. Christian hope grasps that idolatry and unrighteousness can be found at each pole in the culture wars.

Living with an active aspiration for the unshakable kingdom is a call to a different way of being. This way of being will include bearing the reproach of Christ. In four magnificent verses among his final words, the

Pastor lets us know that those who have responded to the grace of God in Jesus Christ and turned to him in faith should not expect to become popular by standing firm in the faith.

> For the bodies of those animals whose blood is brought into the holy places by the high priest as a sacrifice for sin are burned outside the camp. So Jesus also suffered outside the gate in order to sanctify the people through his own blood. Therefore let us go to him outside the camp and bear the reproach he endured. For here we have no lasting city, but we seek the city that is to come. (Hebrews 13:11-14)

These verses are magnificent because he is sparking in their minds that premier day in the Jewish calendar, the Day of Atonement, Yom Kippur. Burnt offerings were not only sacrifices, they were also food for the priests. However, no part of the bull for the sin offering that made atonement for the Holy Place was to be used as a sacrificial meal for the priest. The blood was brought into the Holy Place and the body was taken outside of the camp and completely burned.

The Pastor says this annual ritual was a foreshadowing of Jesus. What we see here is that it wasn't just the sacrifice of the animal itself that pointed to Jesus. The fact that the body was burned outside the camp was just as significant. When Israel was in the wilderness, the land that was "outside of the camp" was unsanctified territory. It was unholy land. Jesus' sacrifice took place outside the gates of Jerusalem on Calvary. This was earth shattering for the Pastor's readers to be told that in order to make people holy, in order to sanctify them through his own blood, Jesus suffered on unholy ground. The very ritual on the Day of Atonement pointed forward to its own end. The burning of the bull's body outside the camp pointed to the fact that to deal with our sin God was going to identify himself with the world in its unholiness.

While we are unable to draw near to God because of our sin, God draws near to us in the person of his Holy One, who on our unholy ground makes his holiness available to us in exchange for our sin which he bears and for which he atones on the cross. The truth of Hebrews 13:10-11 is not just a matter of doctrinal precision. It means something for those who follow Jesus. Since he suffered outside the gate, the message is to let us go out to him, outside the camp to bear his reproach. This cross of Christ, which is the altar of grace and privilege where we are reconciled to God and have peace with God, is located outside the camp. The cross was too shameful to be located inside the gates of Jerusalem. There is an unavoidable shame, an unavoidable reproach that comes with belonging to Jesus Christ.

Privilege and persecution are connected. The blood of bulls and goats that was offered inside the camp could never take away sins, but Jesus sanctifies through his own blood. Since neither the sacrifice of his body nor the offering of his blood took place in the camp, his people, who are sanctified, bear his reproach "outside the camp." In fact, they go to him there. They're not looking to be "on the inside" so to speak, accepted and unified with those who have diverse and strange (un-gospel) teachings. Yet at the same time, the call to go out is a call to engage this world in love.

When Christians want to build secure walls, impenetrable holy huddles that protect them from being defiled by the world, you know what happens? We never bear any reproach or persecution because we're always preaching to the choir. It's respectable inside the camp. We get amens inside the camp. We don't risk shame or rejection or suffering or persecution inside the camp. But we're not with Jesus. He got up close and personal with sinners, never for one moment compromising God's holiness or truth. His eyes were merciful and gracious. He didn't isolate himself from sinners because he knew what they needed. But it wasn't safe. It cost him dearly.

"To be human is to care," writes Esther Meek. To be human is not to disconnect from the world, withdrawing into a life of not seeing the brokenness around us. "To be a human is to be situated in a world and oriented toward it, ever reaching beyond where we are, made to care for it. . . . To care is to move toward the unknown in hope."[8] To be oriented toward the world is to be oriented toward blessing in a way that shows the light of the unshakable kingdom today. Care and love are intimately connected. We long to know how our caring will pan out, but we cannot. We know that if we're faithful there will be reproach that looks Christlike.

We also know that Jesus gives us his peace to persevere in this loving care. "Peace I leave with you; my peace I give to you. Not as the world gives do I give to you. Let not your hearts be troubled, neither let them be afraid" (John 14:27). The peace that Jesus gives to his people is intimately related to the Father's sending them the Holy Spirit in Jesus' name (John 14:26). This peace isn't a sense of tranquility or an absence of strife. It is a palpable taste of the world to come, a taste of the kingdom that has broken in on this world, a taste of kingdom shalom, the restoration of all things. This is his promise.

Avail NYC is one of my favorite organizations. They exist "to empower women and men looking for pregnancy help in NYC."[9] In this polarized pro-choice vs. pro-life toxic battle, they refuse to be pigeonholed into a partisan political voice. They describe their story this way,

> Avail NYC was founded in 1996 by a group of seven women and one man who imagined a new way to serve people facing an unexpected pregnancy or abortion experience. Compassion and confidentiality in a strictly non-political environment was the goal of our founders.[10]

They are committed to coming alongside with pregnancy help or postabortion care with compassion and a desire for healing. They've discarded the partisan labels of our political rhetoric. And do you know what that has resulted in? They get criticized and vilified by those who are unable to fit them into their partisan box. And they are committed to persevering, bearing that reproach.

Living with active aspiration for the unshakable kingdom means that we will bear the reproach of Christ because we won't fit neatly into the boxes or echo chambers that the world creates. In Luke 7, Jesus condemns the leaders of his generation who rejected John the Baptist's ascetic ministry along with his own ministry of abundance. He said they were like children sitting in the marketplace calling to one another, "We played the flute for you, and you did not dance. We sang a dirge, and you did not weep" (7:31-32). Why did they reject John's asceticism on one hand and call Jesus a glutton and drunkard on the other? Because the priorities of the unshakable kingdom do not look like the priorities of this world.

Jesus bore reproach because his message was not comfortable and did not conform to the acceptable teaching of the day. His people will, therefore, also bear reproach because they carry his same message. Yet they endure because they understand that here they do not have an abiding city. They seek after the city that is to come—home.

Have you ever been lost and found your way home? My father was an accountant, and he worked at the World Trade Center for part of his career. It wasn't until I was a middle school student that my parents began to let me take the train by myself. The bus, yes, but not the train. There was a school event in Manhattan that my parents and my sister and I were planning to attend. I was to meet my father at the World Trade Center train station. He and I would then travel together to the event and meet my mother and sister.

My parents gave me instructions on the train to take from our home, where to transfer to another line along with where and what time to meet my father. I got on the correct train from my home and transferred to the correct line at the correct station. However, when I transferred to the correct line, I took the train going in the wrong direction! Well on my way to the Bronx instead of lower Manhattan, I was lost and confused. Of course, if I wasn't so rattled, I would have caught my breath, gotten off the train, and gone back in the other direction. But I was frozen except for the tears streaming down my face. This was well before the days of cell phones or even pagers. A woman saw me crying and asked me what was wrong. I explained what happened and she gave me the exact instructions to retrace my steps.

I made it to the World Trade Center station close to two hours past the time my parents were expecting me. Since I was coming from the opposite direction, I was on the platform across from where I was to meet my father. By this time, my mother was there as well. There they were standing together across the tracks. I couldn't know then, but I certainly know now as a parent the absolute fear and anxiety they would've been feeling. I did not know whether my father would still be there. But where else would he be? When I saw them, my fears vanished. I was still in the train station, but I knew I was going to make it home. They yelled from across the tracks with joy and relief, "Don't move!" I was all too happy to oblige. I was secure. Trains were still taking passengers in the opposite direction, but that didn't matter. Home was in view, and I was guaranteed to get there.

That feeling of calm, relief, joy, and security that comes after you've been lost and have home in view is the liberation we are gifted by God. The Pastor said that Abraham was looking for a city with foundations, whose designer and builder is God (11:13). Now he says that we are seeking that same city as we care for the one we live in today. The world is full of chaos and the storms that shake the world are contrasted with the kingdom that cannot be shaken. Christian hope is liberating in this way. Because of our freedom, we engage the issues of our wearying world in love.

One of our church's favorite songs is "In Jesus' Name" by Israel Houghton and Darlene Zschech. There is such joy and celebration when we sing these words:

> God is fighting for us
> Pushing back the darkness
> Lighting up the Kingdom
> That cannot be shaken

God delights in lighting up the kingdom as his people persevere in hope, demonstrating his love as we anticipate the day when all peoples, nations, and languages will serve the king (Daniel 7:13-14). Hope isn't a hustle, not because of us, but because of God. God's persistence and his commitment is why Christian hope isn't a hustle, but a secure anchor in a wearying world.

"May the God of hope fill you with all joy and peace in believing, so that by the power of the Holy Spirit you may abound in hope" (Romans 15:13).

NOTES

INTRODUCTION: HUSTLING OR HOPING?

[1] Barna Group, "Americans Struggle to Talk Across Divides," March 9, 2016.

[2] Marva J. Dawn, *Unfettered Hope: A Call to Faithful Living in an Affluent Society* (Louisville, KY: Westminster John Knox Press, 2003), xii.

1. LIVING IN THE DANGER ZONE

[1] Greg Glassman, "What Is Fitness?," *The CrossFit Journal*, no. 3 (October 2002): 2, http://library.crossfit.com/free/pdf/CFJ-trial.pdf?_ga=2.22540926.459611967.164 4171943-1050440636.1644171943.

[2] Greg Glassman, "Benchmark Workouts," *The CrossFit Journal*, no. 13 (September 2003): 5, http://library.crossfit.com/free/pdf/13_03_Benchmark_Workouts.pdf.

[3] Glassman, "Benchmark Workouts."

[4] The text of Hebrews itself does not provide the name of its author. A seminary professor of mine was the first person I encountered who used the title *Pastor* to describe the author. Gareth Lee Cockrill in *The Epistle to the Hebrews* puts it well when he says of the author, "His deep concern for the spiritual welfare of his hearers, his preoccupation with the OT, and the sermonic shape of his book . . . justify our referring to him as 'the pastor.'" Gareth Lee Cockerill, *The Epistle to the Hebrews*, The New International Commentary on the Old and New Testament (Grand Rapids, MI: Eerdmans, 2012), 3.

[5] Ernst Hoffman, "Hope, Expectation," in *New International Dictionary of the New Testament*, ed. Colin Brown (Grand Rapids, MI: Zondervan, 1986), electronic ed., 2:241.

[6] Robert J. Cara, "Covenant in Hebrews," in *Covenant Theology: Biblical, Theological, and Historical Perspectives*, ed. Guy Prentiss Waters, J. Nicholas Reid, and John R. Muether (Wheaton, IL: Crossway, 2020), 247-48.

[7] There will be much more to come on the connection between Jesus' priesthood and the certainty of our hope later in the book.

[8] Isaac Watts, "When I Survey the Wondrous Cross," 1707.

2. CONSIDERING JESUS IN THE DANGER ZONE

[1] Bruce Bryant-Scott, "Herbert's Dialogue with Hope," *The Island Parson* blog, April 10, 2019, https://theislandparson.com/2019/04/10/herberts-dialogue-with-hope/.

[2] Martin Luther King Jr., "Shattered Dreams," in *The Strength to Love* (Boston: Beacon Press Books, 1981), 89-90.

[3] King Jr., "Shattered Dreams," 92.

[4] Herman Bavinck, *Reformed Dogmatics: Holy Spirit, Church, and New Creation*, ed. John Bolt, trans. John Vriend, (Grand Rapids, MI: Baker Academic, 2008), 4:715.

[5] Barna Group, *The Open Generation*, vol. 1, *How Teens Around the World Relate to Jesus* (Ventura, CA: Barna Group, 2022), 6.

[6] Barna Group, *Open Generation*, vol. 1, 10.

[7] Barna Group, *Open Generation*, vol. 1, 10.

[8] Barna Group, *Open Generation*, vol. 1, 22-24.

[9] Barna Group, *Open Generation*, vol. 1, 30.

3. RESTING IN THE DANGER ZONE

[1] Alicia J. Akins, *Invitations to Abundance* (Eugene, OR: Harvest House Publishers, 2022), 64.

[2] Gregory Thompson, "Love in the Streets: The Faith-Based Civil Rights Movement and the Contemporary Church," Grace Mosaic Fall Lecture Series, October 2021, https://youtu.be/RgpBycS0zRs, unlisted.

[3] Thompson, "Love in the Streets."

[4] Philip Edgcumbe Hughes, *A Commentary on the Epistle to the Hebrews*, The New International Commentary on the Old and New Testament (Grand Rapids, MI: Eerdmans, 1977), 155.

[5] See Isaiah 55:10-11; 2 Timothy 3:15-17; 2 Peter 1:20-21.

[6] William Hendriksen, *John*, Hendriksen & Kistemaker New Testament Commentary (Grand Rapids, MI: Baker, 1953), 2:365.

4. THE UNREASONABLE HOPE

[1] R. B. Jamieson, *The Paradox of Sonship: Christology in the Epistle to the Hebrews*, Studies in Christian Doctrine and Scripture (Downers Grove, IL: IVP Academic, 2021), 147.

[2] "So what I want to do is examine our society as secular in this . . . sense, which I could perhaps encapsulate in this way: the change I want to define and trace is one which takes us from a society in which it was virtually impossible not to believe in God, to one in which faith, even for the staunchest believer, is one human possibility among others, including possibly some very close to me, whose way of living I cannot in all

honesty just dismiss as depraved, or blind, or unworthy, who have no faith (at least not in God, or the transcendent). Belief in God is no longer axiomatic. There are alternatives. And this will also likely mean that at least in certain milieux, it may be hard to sustain one's faith. There will be people who feel bound to give it up, even though they mourn its loss. This has been a recognizable experience in our societies, at least since the mid-nineteenth century. There will be many others to whom faith never even seems an eligible possibility. There are certainly millions today of whom this is true." Charles Taylor, *A Secular Age* (Cambridge, MA: Harvard University Press, 2007), 3.

[3] David T. Koyzis, *Political Visions & Illusions: A Survey and Christian Critique of Contemporary Ideologies* (Downers Grove, IL: InterVarsity Press, 2007), 2.

5. THE PERFECT HOPE

[1] He's quoted from Genesis 2, 22; Deuteronomy 32; 2 Samuel 7; Psalms 2, 8, 22, 45, 95, 102, 104, 110; and Isaiah 8.

[2] Sermon preached by Rev. Russ Whitfield, "The Day of Atonement," October 24, 2021, Grace Mosaic Church, https://gracemosaic.org/sermon-audio/the-day-of -atonement.

[3] Philip Edgcumbe Hughes, *A Commentary on the Epistle to the Hebrews*, The New International Commentary on the Old and New Testament (Grand Rapids, MI: Eerdmans, 1977), 254-55.

[4] Today, fentanyl overdoses are the leading cause of accidental deaths in the United States in people under sixty-five years old. Dr. Peter Attia, "Improve Vitality, Emotional & Physical Health & Lifespan," *Huberman Lab* podcast, March 20, 2023, https:// youtu.be/ufsIA5NARIo.

[5] Terry Gross, "Remembering Michael K. Williams," NPR, September 8, 2021, www .npr.org/2021/09/08/1035141850/remembering-michael-k-williams.

6. THE BETTER HOPE

[1] Jeremy Renner plays the character Hawkeye in the Marvel movies and TV series.

[2] "Jeremy Renner: The Diane Sawyer Interview—A Story of Terror, Survival and Triumph," directed by Dave Hoffman, aired April 6, 2023, on ABC.

[3] Elissa Epel, *The Stress Prescription* (New York: Penguin Books, 2022), 28.

[4] Epel, *Stress Prescription*, 30.

[5] Chris Bail, *Breaking the Social Media Prism: How to Make Our Platforms Less Polarizing* (Princeton, NJ: Princeton University Press, 2021), 10.

[6] Philip Edgcumbe Hughes, *A Commentary on the Epistle to the Hebrews*, The New International Commentary on the Old and New Testament (Grand Rapids, MI: Eerdmans, 1977), 300.

7. REMEMBER TO ENDURE

[1] Gerard Manley Hopkins, "Pied Beauty," Poetry Foundation, www.poetryfoundation .org/poems/44399/pied-beauty.

[2] David Zucchino, *Wilmington's Lie: The Murderous Coup of 1898 and the Rise of White Supremacy* (New York: Atlantic Monthly Press, 2020), 262.

[3] Zucchino, *Wilmington's Lie*, 263.

[4] Zucchino, *Wilmington's Lie*, 263.

[5] Philip Edgcumbe Hughes, *A Commentary on the Epistle to the Hebrews*, The New International Commentary on the Old and New Testament (Grand Rapids, MI: Eerdmans, 1977), 433.

8. PERSEVERE BY FAITH

[1] Frances Perraudin, "Manchester University Students Paint Over Rudyard Kipling Mural," *The Guardian*, July 19, 2018, www.theguardian.com/education/2018/jul/19 /manchester-university-students-paint-over-rudyard-kipling-mural.

[2] Rudyard Kipling, "If—," Poetry Foundation, www.poetryfoundation.org/poems /46473/if---.

[3] Kipling, "If—"

[4] Omnibrain, "How Superman's X-Ray Vision Works," *ScienceBlogs*, October 5, 2009, https://scienceblogs.com/omnibrain/2009/10/05/how-supermans-x-ray -vision-wor#google_vignette.

[5] *The Karate Kid*, directed by Harald Zwart (Culver City, CA: Columbia Pictures, 2010).

[6] Philip Edgcumbe Hughes, *A Commentary on the Epistle to the Hebrews*, The New International Commentary on the Old and New Testament (Grand Rapids, MI: Eerdmans, 1977), 439.

[7] Raymond C. Barfield, "Seeing the Beauty of Dappled Things: Gerard Manley Hopkins," *Comment* magazine, Winter 2017, 27, https://comment.org/seeing-the -beauty-of-dappled-things-gerard-manley-hopkins/.

[8] Barfield, "Seeing."

[9] Barfield, "Seeing."

[10] Barfield, "Seeing."

[11] Elissa Yukiko Weichbrodt, *Redeeming Vision: A Christian Guide to Looking at and Learning from Art* (Grand Rapids, MI: Baker Academic, 2023), 19.

9. LIVE FOR THE CITY

[1] John Cotton, "God's Promise to His Plantation," London, 1630.

[2] Stevie Wonder, "Living for the City," by Stevie Wonder, *Innervisions*, Tamla, 1973.

[3] Augustine of Hippo, *The City of God, Books VIII–XVI,* ed. Hermigild Dressler, trans. Gerald G. Walsh and Grace Monahan, The Fathers of the Church (Washington, DC: The Catholic University of America Press, 1952), 14:467.

[4] John M. Frame, *The Doctrine of God: A Theology of Lordship* (Phillipsburg, NJ: P&R Publishing, 2002), 87.

[5] John Calvin, *Commentary on the Epistle of Paul the Apostle to the Hebrews,* ed. John Owen (Bellingham, WA: Logos Bible Software, 2010), 302-303.

10. RUN THROUGH EXHAUSTION

[1] Jerry Lynch and Warren A. Scott, *Running Within: A Guide to Mastering the Body-Mind-Spirit* (Champaign, IL: Human Kinetics, 1999), 121.

[2] Michael O. Emerson, et al., *Beyond Diversity: What the Future of Racial Justice Will Require of U.S. Churches* (Ventura, CA: Barna Group, 2021), 5.

[3] Emerson, *Beyond Diversity,* 9.

[4] Emerson, *Beyond Diversity,* 6.

[5] The complete list of verses is Matthew 14:3; Acts 7:58; Romans 13:12; Ephesians 4:22, 25; Colossians 3:8; Hebrews 12:1; James 1:21; 1 Peter 2:1.

[6] Geerhardus Vos, *The Teaching of Jesus Concerning the Kingdom of God and the Church* (Grand Rapids, MI: Eerdmans, 1958), 50.

[7] To be clear, when I list pro-choice and pro-life as "false choices," I'm referring to partisan positions. That is, a pro-choice position that says the only way to be pro-woman is to put no limits on abortion. And a pro-life position that is more pro-birth than pro-life—against abortion but not for the social structures necessary for the flourishing of life from the womb to the tomb.

[8] Esther Lightcap Meek, *Loving to Know: Covenant Epistemology* (Eugene, OR: Cascade Books, 2011), 31, Kindle.

[9] "Our Mission," Avail NYC website, accessed April 21, 2023, www.availnyc.org /about-avail-nyc.

[10] "Our Story," Avail NYC website, accessed April 21, 2023, www.availnyc.org /about-avail-nyc.

ALSO BY IRWYN L. INCE JR.

The Beautiful Community
978-0-8308-4831-7